mamma mia!

mamma mia!

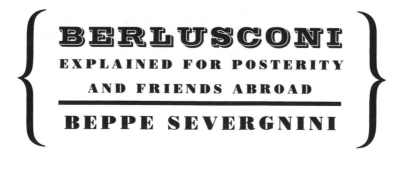

{ **BERLUSCONI**
EXPLAINED FOR POSTERITY
AND FRIENDS ABROAD

BEPPE SEVERGNINI }

Rizzoli
ex libris

First published in the United States of America in 2011
by Rizzoli Ex Libris, an imprint of
Rizzoli International Publications, Inc.
300 Park Avenue South
New York, NY 10010
www.rizzoliusa.com

Originally appeared in Italy as
La Pancia Degli Italiani: Berlusconi Spiegato Ai Posteri.
Copyright © 2010 by RCS Libri S.p.A. Milano

Translated by Giles Watson

This edition published by arrangement with Georges Borchardt, Inc., New York,
and Rosaria Carpinelli Consulenze Editoriali srl., Milano

2011 2012 2013 2014 / 10 9 8 7 6 5 4 3 2 1

Distributed in the U.S. trade by Random House, New York

Printed in the United States of America

ISBN-13: 978-0-8478-3741-0

Library of Congress Catalog Control Number: 2011930248

To his electors and disrespecters

I'm not afraid of Berlusconi in himself,
I'm afraid of Berlusconi in me.
GIAN PIERO ALLOISIO

Contents

Ten Factors (Plus One)

Explaining Silvio Berlusconi to the Italians is a waste of time. Everyone has a take, honed by years of indulgence or intolerance, and impervious to change. Every Italian has the one true interpretation. Discussion is superfluous.

Profiling Silvio Berlusconi for posterity, and for non-Italians while we're at it, will be more helpful. The future isn't here yet, but it will want to know what was going on, and non-Italians just don't get it, but would like to.

How was it that Silvio Berlusconi—Mr. B. for short—was voted into power (1994), voted in again (2001), and voted back in (2008)? The hammerings he took in the administrative elections and referendum (2011) hint at change, but the question remains: Why does a majority of Italians support and/or put up with him? Can't they see his appetites, his limits, his methods? Obviously, they can. If Mr. B. has dominated public life for almost two decades, there is a reason. Actually, there are ten (plus one).

1. THE HUMAN FACTOR

What do most Italians think about Silvio Berlusconi? "He's just like us." And the ones who don't are afraid he might be. Mr. B. adores his kids, talks about his *mamma*, knows his soccer, makes money, loves new homes, hates rules, tells jokes, uses bad language, adores women, parties hard, and is convivial to a fault. He has a good memory and a knack for tactical amnesia. He's come a long way, switching between life's freeways and its shortcuts. He's unconventional, but knows the importance of convention. He extols the Church in the morning and the family in the afternoon, and brings girlfriends home in the evening.

Mr. B. is great entertainment value, so he gets away with plenty. Many Italians ignore his conflicts of interest (haven't we all got 'em?), his legal issues (a defendant is easier to like than a judge), and his international bloopers (he's so spontaneous!). What about the broken promises, the half truths, the blurring of public and private life? Some people get worked up about that sort of thing; others turn a blind eye. Apparently, there are more of the latter than the former.

2. THE DIVINE FACTOR

Mr. B. knows that praising the Church helps most Italians feel less guilty about not going to mass, or systematically ignoring seven of the ten commandments. We don't expect our leaders to walk the walk when they talk the talk. Private indignation at public contradictions shifts votes in many democracies, but not in Italy. Silvio knows that he's dealing with a country that eschews expectations to avoid disappointment.

The Vatican, if not Italy's parishes, is content with Catholicism-friendly legislation and doesn't worry about the bad examples. Catholic movements such as Comunione e Liberazione like to focus on ends, which are safely in the future and therefore negotiable, rather than the means their friends employ to reach them. This eschatological take is music to Mr. B.'s ears, for it shifts attention from actions to intentions.

3. THE ROBINSON FACTOR

Every Italian feels he or she stands alone against the world, or if not the world, the neighbors. We take pride in surviving, socially and economically. It shows how resourceful we are. Much has been written about Italian individualism, its expedients, its limitations, and its consequences. Mr. B. started out from there, first amassing his fortune and establishing himself as a self-made man, before building on Italy's distrust of all things shared, the widespread antipathy for rules, and the inner satisfaction Italians take in finding a private solution to a public problem. In Italy, there is no real cohesive public pressure for a new, fairer tax system. People evade the one they have.

Every Italian feels like Robinson Crusoe, a castaway on a crowded peninsula.

4. THE TRUMAN FACTOR

How many newspapers, apart from sports papers, are sold in Italy every day? Five million. How many Italians regularly use bookstores? Five million. How many Italians browse major news websites? Five million. How many watch the Sky TG24 and TG La7 news? Five million. How many watch current affairs programs on late-evening television? Five million, across the political spectrum.

You get the feeling they're always the same people, so we'll call them the Five Million Club. Are they important? Obviously, but they don't decide elections. Television—all TV, not just newscasts—remains pivotal, because it molds images, sends out messages, leaves impressions, tells you some things and, crucially, keeps quiet about others. Guess who owns private television and controls public TV in Italy.

It's like Peter Weir's seminal film, *The Truman Show*. Someone helped us think.

5. *THE HOOVER FACTOR*

Hoover, founded in 1908 in New Berlin (now Canton) in Ohio, is synonymous with vacuum cleaners. In English-speaking countries, to use a vacuum cleaner is simply "to hoover." The company's door-to-door reps were skillful, legendarily tenacious manipulators of psychology, ruthless in pursuit of a sale.

Mr. B. has a flair for commercial seduction, carried over from his previous careers in construction, television, and advertising, that he now applies to politics. He's well aware that a message has to be straightforward, appealing, and reassuring. He knows that repeating it works. And he is convinced that in an appearance-obsessed nation, image is key. In Italy, making the right impression wins hands down over doing the right thing.

6. *THE ZELIG FACTOR*

All politicians need to be able to identify with their interlocutors. Few are capable of actually turning into them. A need for approval has taught Mr. B. the art of transformation. Woody Allen's Zelig would be proud. A family man with his five children (and two wives, while they lasted). A women's man among the ladies. Youthful with the young. Wise with the old. A night owl with the night set. A worker at the workplace. Entrepreneurial with the business community. Youthful with the young. *Rossonero* to the core with A.C. Milan supporters. Milanese with the people of Milan.

Lombard with the people of Lombardy. Italian with people from southern Italy. A Neapolitan among Neapolitans (and their music). If he went to see a basketball game, he'd walk out taller.

7. THE HAREM FACTOR

Silvio's obsession with women, an open secret in his business circles and then in Rome's corridors of power, became public knowledge in 2009, when he attended Noemi Letizia's eighteenth birthday party and reports emerged about his soirées at Villa Certosa and Palazzo Grazioli. At first, he denied the charges, then he grudgingly admitted them ("Am I faithful? Frequently."), and in the end he played along ("I'm no saint."). The revelations left him unscathed. He lost his wife, but not his electoral base. Lots of Italians who prefer self-indulgence to self-discipline admit that Mr. B. does what they can only dream of doing. But there's more to this than titillation. Youth is contagious, as they knew in ancient Greece (where pretty young things of both sexes took advantage to learn from the old). One staunch, long-term associate, now in his sixties, has described how restless Silvio gets during marathon meetings: "It's clear he's afraid he'll catch old age from us."

8. THE MEDICI FACTOR

Together with the *comune*, or municipality, the *signoria* (absolute lordship) is the only original political unit Italians have created. All the others, from feudalism to monarchy, totalitarianism, federalism, and parliamentary democracy, have been imported from France, Britain, Germany, Spain, or the United States. Their Italian incarnations have always been slightly artificial—take Fascism's cringe-making awkwardness, or the acquiescence of today's Parliament—but a *signoria* stirs ancient instincts.

The attitudes of many Italians toward Mr. B. are reminiscent of how their forebears regarded the *signore*, or lord. We know he puts his own glory, family, and interests ahead of everything else, but we hope he'll spare a thought for us. Giuseppe Prezzolini noted, "The fact that they had to lead such difficult lives, made of the *signori* keen observers of men." Cosimo de' Medici, founder of the great Florentine dynasty, is reported to have been circumspect and capable of reading a man's character merely by looking at him. Silvio Berlusconi is also regarded as a formidable connoisseur of men, by whom he demands to be admired, not criticized; adulated, not betrayed; and loved, not weighed in the balance.

9. THE T.I.N.A. FACTOR

T.I.N.A.: There Is No Alternative. Margaret Thatcher's classic acronym says it all about many voters. The Center-Left alternative to Mr. B. has proved unappetizing—strife-torn coalitions, woolly ideas, and hypocritical behavior—and the Democratic Party's communist origins are undeniable, as Mr. B. never fails to underline. When in power, Italy's Center-Left has had spectacular, carbon-copy failures: elected in 1996 and 2006, only to commit suicide in 1998 and 2008.

Italians are pragmatic. Before selecting what they think is right, they take what seems useful. And some of Mr. B.'s initiatives are popular, or at least less unpopular than the alternative: abolition of the local property tax on first homes, discouraging illegal immigration, the fight against organized crime, and reforming traffic law. If these initiatives are successful, there are plenty of media channels happy to remind us of the fact. Should they flop, someone will help us to forget.

It also has to be said that a united Center-Right is at least as reassuring as a divided Center-Left is irritating. If the only way to keep a political alliance together is to own it, Mr. B. was swift to work out how much it would cost: financially, politically, and in frayed nerves. Without realizing it, Mr. B. followed the advice of President Lyndon B. Johnson, who said, apropos of F.B.I. chief J. Edgar Hoover, "It's probably better to have him inside the tent pissing out, than outside the tent pissing in." This accounts for Mr. B.'s expulsion of, and disdain for, Gianfranco Fini, cofounder of the People of Freedom. In 2010, Mr. Fini dared to leave the tent after sixteen years without indicating which way he would be pointing.

10. THE PALIO FACTOR

You've probably heard about the Palio horse race in Siena. For the winning *contrada*, as the competing districts of the city are called, it is a huge source of satisfaction. But it's equally satisfying when your most hated rival *contrada* loses. Lots of things work like that in Italy, from geography to industry, the arts, and sports. Lazio soccer fans, for instance, were delighted to lose to Inter Milan so that capital city rivals A.S. Roma would not be champions. Politics is no exception. Tribalism is not a tactic; it's an instinct. To keep the left they see as unreliable out of power, many Italians would have voted for the Devil. And Mr. B. can be pretty diabolical. But Satan's style is something else.

Okay, now let's take a closer look at these ten factors (plus one).

{ **CHAPTER ONE** }

The Human Factor

e was showing the girls some videos. Steamy sex? No, just clips from the news. That was him strolling with George W. Bush at Camp David. The three women stared at the screen, concentrating like schoolgirls who would be quizzed later. Two asked to go to the rest room. They fixed their hair and took souvenir photos in front of the mirror.[1] Otherwise, who would believe them?

Palazzo Grazioli is a ravishing Roman residence, rich in history and previously owned by Jesuits, architects, ambassadors, princesses, barons, and knights. Who among them would have imagined that the tenant on the first floor—furnished by Giorgio Pes, who designed sets for Luchino

Visconti—would be organizing a film show? Not for counsel-ors, ministers, or industrialists. No, for young women forced, by their status and circumstances, to express amazement. This is showing off so ingenuous as to be disarming.

Why are we starting here? The episode helps us to understand how Mr. B. has been seducing Italians for years—by behaving like them. Not all Italians, but enough of them to secure a majority, with a little help from a favor-able election law. Palazzo Grazioli is on Via del Plebiscito, or Plebiscite Street, an address that reflects a dream and, at least for the first part of the evening, our hero was seek-ing approval. By showing films and photos of his villas. Only later would he invite the chosen female to wait for him in "Putin's bed," one trophy tucked up in another to show off to a nonexistent audience. The dogged exuber-ance of a man who, like so many others, refuses to grow old. Unlike almost everyone else, though, he thinks he knows how not to.

Mr. B. is the updated autobiography of a nation,[2] and autobiographies abound with self-indulgence and omissions. Tens of millions of Italians ignore his conflicts of interest (haven't we all got 'em?), his broken promises (we all break 'em), the tailor-made laws (he can get away with it!), and his legal issues (it could be us tomorrow). What about the half truths, the unanswered questions? Well, "accountabil-ity" is hard to translate into Italian. And *simpatia* has no real equivalent in English.

A good way to garner *simpatia*—by accident, design, or error—is to get down with the less well-informed voters. Aw-shucks moments. In May 2010, Mr. B. said at a media briefing at Villa Madama: "We have so many technological tools. What with Gogol and other Internet resources."[3] Gogol? Nikolai Vasilievich? The Russian writer? Ah, but perhaps he meant Google, the search engine. Mr. B. is unfamiliar with the Internet. In 2009, he asked the head of a leading IT company: "Excuse me, but do you know what the Internet is for?"[4] Proof of inadequacy? In other countries, perhaps. In Italy, there is a part of the electorate that, like Mr. B., doesn't surf the Net, but does vote. And they're people who like to feel they're not alone.

The same goes for his bloopers on official occasions, in Italy and abroad. They are not necessarily counterproductive.

In the past eight years, Mr. B. has managed to:

- make the "horns" hand gesture in an official photograph (2002);

- tell a member of the European parliament that he would put him forward "for the role of *kapo*," a prisoner put in charge of the other prisoners, in a "film on concentration camps" (2003);

- get himself photographed next to Tony Blair while wearing a bandana on his head (2004);

- raise his middle finger during a rally (2005);

- reveal that he "dusted off his prowess as a playboy" with the Finnish president Tarja Halonen (2005);

- maintain that Maoists in China "boiled babies to fertilize the fields" (2006);

- parade A.C. Milan's Brazilian soccer players in front of President Luiz Inácio Lula da Silva as if they were baseball cards (2008);

- play hide-and-seek with Angela Merkel (2008);

- make said German chancellor stand and wait for him on the red carpet while he was speaking on his cell phone (2009);

- irritate Queen Elizabeth II by shouting at other guests (2009);

- claim he "told" the American and Russian presidents to sign the nuclear arms reduction treaty (2010).[5]

The foreign press snickers,[6] and the Web regularly ridicules him,[7] but a good slice of Italian public opinion smiles. Human, so very human.

Mr. B.'s success is too enduring to be a coincidence. He prevails by complicity, not example or authority. I am like you: impulsive, intolerant, enthusiastic, and impatient.

I am prepared to admit my own weaknesses and forgive yours. I keep guilt at arm's length. Or admit it, if there's no comeback.

Telling a joke about Nazi death camps just before the Holocaust Day of Memory is—at best—poor timing, and reeling off another two about Hitler and tight-fisted Jews looks like appalling taste.[8] Anti-Semitic? Not at all. Calling Barack Obama "handsome, young, and suntanned"[9] is bizarre, and offensive for many people. But is it racist? Certainly not. In both cases, Mr. B. is a victim of the desire to please, which induces people in general, and Italians in particular, to go too far.

Presented with episodes like these, the Left attempts to depict Mr. B. as irresponsible, while the Right tries to make him out as a victim of other people's skullduggery. Yet he is neither one thing nor the other.

Silvio's spontaneity is calculated. Buoyed up by awesome self-esteem, probably a reaction to some deep-seated insecurity, Mr. B. struts with a genuine swagger. He isn't putting it on. He has a formidable instinct and understands that criticism abroad, and the embarrassment of some Italians, boost his popularity with ordinary people. The folks who used to vote for the Left and now prefer him.

Having said whatever he felt like, as his advisers hung their heads and his admirers' eyes misted over, Silvio in effect discovered there was a political edge to be gained. Barroom humor? Well, elections are won in barrooms, not think tanks. Only the éminence gris of the Left, Massimo D'Alema, fails to see this.

Mr. B. is Italy talking from the gut. He's a ventriloquist who gets away with plenty.

On September 24, 2003, he stunned Wall Street when he said one of the reasons for bringing investment capital to Italy was that "We have great-looking secretaries, fantastic girls. Try investing in Italy, where you can do so in a blissful atmosphere."[10] Did he realize that he was in the United States, where you can end up in court over a remark like that? Perhaps he did. But fear of upsetting the other person is always overridden by the desire to impress.

Attractive secretaries as rewards for long service and relief from the monotony of the office filled Italian comedies and films for decades, and continue to feature in advertising, aspirations, and speeches. A certain enduring male mindset lurks just below society's radar. Hidden in a glance, nuanced into a casual remark, kicking its shoes off in the office cafeteria at lunchtime as colleagues swap fantasies, ready to lower their eyes if the smiling object of their desires approaches. Mr. B. knows this.

On February 12, 2010, the Italian prime minister met Albania's premier Sali Berisha. "I don't want any more bodies in the Channel of Otranto. I don't want flows of criminals to Italy," Mr. Berisha said to the press. "Well, we can make the odd exception for pretty girls . . ." said his host.[11] Connecting "flows of criminals to Italy" with pretty

Albanian girls, who are often the criminals' victims, seems irresponsible. With that remark, Mr. B. offered absolution to millions of Italians unsure whether to feel tempted or sorry as they cruise past a woman from Eastern Europe at the side of the road.

Silvio's strong point is flaunting his wealth, not being rich. Wealth engenders envy, but showing it off creates curiosity, and curiosity entertains. That's why monarchies endure, and Hollywood stars are successful. Mr. B. offers an Italian-made version in a never-predictable daily entertainment.

His numerous, opulently appointed residences flaunt tropical gardens, simulated volcanic eruptions, and bathing nymphets. Villa Certosa at Porto Rotondo in Sardinia has been endlessly extended, made over, and touched up into every nouveau riche's erotic property dream. If the neighbors, such as controversial Bari-based entrepreneur Giampaolo Tarantini, tended to bring around rather more than a cute smile and a tub of ice cream, the public has forgotten about it. But the public never forgets the in-your-face behavior associated with power, and is secretly envious.

Mr. B. knows this, and adapts. "The Left keeps telling people to send Berlusconi home, which causes me a certain embarrassment [pauses]. Because I have twenty homes, and I wouldn't know which one to go to."[12] It's not a bad one-liner, but in what other democracy could the head of government express such a sentiment?

Understanding the aspirations of your voters, actual or potential, and indulging their desires, even when these are selfish, is not very farsighted, but it does win votes. And while Villa Certosa and Palazzo Grazioli are the stuff of dreams, most people can make a down payment on a more modest home. In its original form, the government's Homes Plan[13] read like a blueprint for construction anarchy. But it is a smart idea in a nation of insatiable home builders (an aerial survey by the territory agency revealed 2,077,048 unregistered buildings).[14]

Are we nibbling Italy to death? Serena, one of my readers, disagrees. She wrote on my "Italians" forum on the Corriere.it website:

> I live in Modena, a city built for the elderly, in a forty square-meter apartment and I would do anything for a small house with a garden and a dog. Who cares about roots in the countryside! . . . I'm all for new, modern buildings at affordable prices. We thirty-somethings will buy the new homes, don't you worry. We'll leave people your age the homes you're already living in, the places you grabbed when you were our age. You put the others in little boxes. All you've given thirty-year-olds is short-term employment and tiny rented apartments. Well, thanks a million.

Serena might not vote for the People of Freedom, but you can be certain that when Mr. B. insists that "we will build new towns for young people"[15]—ignoring transport and territory management issues—she will be all ears.

Many Italians listened to these sound bites:

I don't want to see just one striker up front. That's why I got rid of coach Leonardo. He kept playing Pato wide. You need two strikers and they should play together in attack.

> *(Visiting Milanello, the A.C. Milan training center)*

We will have a law that means Italians will be unable to speak freely on the telephone.

> *(Milanello again, standing next to A.C. Milan's new coach, Massimiliano Allegri)*

Five children, each one smarter than the last. Credit goes to their parents.

> *(At daughter Barbara's graduation ceremony at the Vita-Salute San Raffaele University in Milan)*

Just minor misunderstandings in the majority.
(At the e-Campus online university in Novedrate, Como)

There's no moral issue in the People of Freedom, just three or four people who are not exactly angelic.

> *(When accepting the Grande Milano award)*

You might ask what parents have got to do with telephones, or the party with A.C. Milan strikers. The answer is easy. The foray, in the space of a few hours on July 19 and 20, 2010, into such widely varying fields had a dual purpose: to show that his worries are the same as everyone else's—children, cell phones, soccer—and to distract attention from the government's problems. The human and the political, eternally intertwined.

Inevitably, Silvio's sound bites filled the newspapers, sports dailies, television news, celebrity mags, blogs, and barroom chitchat. It was a delicate moment. The cofounder of the People of Freedom, Gianfranco Fini, was about to leave the party. Two ministers and a junior minister—Scajola, Brancher, and Cosentino—had resigned. Another junior minister, Giacomo Caliendo, was about to be investigated. The People of Freedom's national coordinator, Denis Verdini, and an old friend of Silvio's, Marcello Dell'Utri, were caught up in a tangle of public contracts and favors. In Center-Right-dominated Lombardy, explanations were required for organized crime worming its way into the healthcare service. Any other head of government would have addressed Parliament, but Silvio spoke to Milanello and the spires of the Milan cathedral.

Every phrase struck a chord in the Italian soul: soccer-related summer fantasizing, antipathy for controls, a parent's pride, and a tendency to play things down. A few days earlier, Mr. B. had spoken to a gathering of the business community, brushing aside judicial investigations as "just a storm in a teacup. I am relaxed. So the papers are talking about a P3 conspiracy? [An allusion to the notorious P2 masonic lodge —Ed.] That's just a handful of sad pensioners who have clubbed together to change Italy. And if

I can't change it . . ."[16] Sad pensioners? That doesn't seem like the best way to describe the individuals arrested or placed under investigation. So what? Pensioners, many only bored, are part of the Italian townscape. They sit in bars or stroll around, waiting for a friendly smile from a passing shop assistant, or for lunchtime to come around. Italians have a soft spot for pensioners. No one could possibly find them intimidating.

Mr. B.'s enemies underestimate the Human Factor. Humanity is neither coherent or predictable. Humanity looks for footholds and excuses. It sneaks in and slithers out, playing off heart against head. But it has more appeal than Virtue.

Besides, Mr. B. has plenty of virtues of his own. He can be generous and loyal with friends, collaborators, and subordinates (in his case, the three categories tend to overlap). His trademarks are what Natalia Ginzburg, who distrusted them, called the "little virtues:"[17] cunning instead of love of truth; diplomacy instead of love for your neighbor; and a desire, not for being or knowing, but for success. One more detail: These little virtues are shared by the great majority of Italians.

Being human means dreaming like everyone else, and buying dreams not everyone else can afford. Edmondo Berselli wrote at the start of the new millennium, "Some Italians had to make a huge effort to shake off the weight of ideology . . . Many others changed lifestyle, mentality, and in some cases their look, with the ethical and aesthetic relief that accompanies a coming-out when you finally reveal what you have always been deep down in your soul."[18]

The often hypocritical pedagogic zeal, which did at least keep the lid on Italy's national instincts, was replaced by publicly paraded pleasure-seeking.

It may not have been "one of the most spectacular mutations experienced by a modern community," but there is no denying that a change took place. We might not have witnessed the "emancipation of the nation's animal spirit,"[19] but there is an atavistic, knee-jerk quality to certain reactions to power. Perhaps it wasn't a "no longer censorious representation of Italians' desires as they really are," yet today's Italians are not those of thirty years ago.

Most, raised on advertising, television, and surgically enhanced celebs, are unperturbed that Mr. B. refuses to grow old. His unchanging face is a mirror that allows us to pretend that we might not change either. The nips, tucks, transplants, and makeup are neither sinful nor embarrassing. Mr. B. extracted solidarity by turning a guilty secret into a proud boast.[20]

According to Italo Calvino, Benito Mussolini transformed baldness from a defect into a mark of virility. Every day, Mr. B. attempts to compensate for being short, chubby, and bald. What the surgeon or the makeup artist can't correct is dealt with by the Berlusconi-owned or controlled media. In Italy, opinions come and go but impressions endure. If anyone seeing him thinks, "He certainly doesn't look his age," Silvio has won.

In summer 2010, there was a rumor that the most plausible and tenacious of his aspiring successors, economy minister Giulio Tremonti, referred to him as "the little granddad" in private.[21] Be warned. When no one is expecting it, Mr. B. could stop dyeing his hair, abandon his belly and the bags under his eyes to gravity, and proclaim himself the father of the fatherland. That's when we'd find him in the Quirinale Palace as president of Italy.

As usual, his enemies would be asking themselves how he got there.

CHAPTER TWO

The Divine Factor

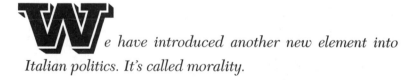*e have introduced another new element into Italian politics. It's called morality.*

He went on to explain further. Morality means not just not stealing ("An important new development that we introduced"). "The new morality," he announced, closing the first Festival of Freedom in Milan on September 27, 2009, "is keeping your election promises."[1]

It's a simplistic definition that enrages detractors, reassures supporters, and leaves everyone else cold. There's no moral vote in Italy, just as there is no Catholic vote. There are votes cast by Catholics, who in theory make up almost the entire population, but in practice, these are split across tens of millions of individual faiths, one for each conscience. As we shall see, those consciences stretch to survive. Silvio knows Italian consciences well. In fact, he has an extremely elastic one of his own.

Why, then, did the Divine Factor assist his ascent and ensure his enduring elevation? Because Italy has an ancient religion, a new religion, a practical religion, and a disoriented religion, all pushing in the same direction.

There is also another religion—the kind that fills lives and warms hearts—shut away in parish recreation centers, convents, local churches, and missions. This religion doesn't know who to vote for, but it does know who not to believe.

There's an ancient religion in Italy, built on tradition, sensitive to evocation, anxious for consolation, and bound to a devotion that in some cases can shade into superstition.

Christianity is no longer a civic religion, as it was in the Italy of the communes. No longer is it an imperial religion, as it was in the Renaissance. It is not the binding force of common folk and the countryside, as it was until the mid-twentieth century. It is not a vote repository, as it was when Christian Democracy was in power. It's not even a social practice any longer. In the—theoretically—ultra-Catholic Veneto region, attendance at services plummeted from seventy-five percent to fifteen percent in thirty years. But religion has conserved its elemental value of protection,[2] as certain people well understand.

Early religious allusions coincided with Mr. B.'s entry into politics. They cropped up in television programs aimed at an audience that has little to do with politics. On January 27, 1994, a very young, remote-controlled,[3] Ambra Angiolini was hosting the show *Non è la Rai* on Italia 1. Discussing A.C. Milan with a devil in a red and black Milan shirt, she commented, "The Lord supports Berlusconi!" And on January 31: "Forza Italiaaa! ['Go, Italy,' the name of Berlusconi's then-new party. —Ed.] Yes, because He, excuse me, is happy about Forza Italia. The Lord supports Forza Italia. And we all know that Satan sticks up for Occhetto [Democratic Left Party secretary, Achille. —Ed.]. Oh, excuse me. And for Stalin, but he's a real weirdo."

The program's author and remote controller, Gianni Boncompagni, played it down as "just a bit of mischief. We're a wonderfully anarchic country." It would be interesting to know what would have happened in this wonderfully anarchic country to his program if the jesting juxtaposition had been the other way round, with the Lord on the side of his opponent, and Satan standing by the proprietor.

In the aftermath of the election victory of March 27 to 28, 1994, the first Berlusconi government acquired a soundtrack with a mystical theme. Pierluigi Battista pointed out, "Having drained the 'bitter chalice,' invoked a new Italian 'miracle,' invited his followers to give thanks for a 'new, magical present,' and insisted, absolutely insisted, that the Forza Italia anthem should contain the line 'we all have a fire in our heart,' Silvio Berlusconi today has no compunction about donning the robes of a new Messiah. 'He who has been chosen by the people is like the Lord's Anointed.' A man chosen in the name of God, which in this case at least is called the People. 'There is something divine about the citizen who chooses his leader.'"[4]

The spiritual appeals of the Salesian Fathers' former pupil don't convince everyone. In August 1994, Catholic scholar Vittorio Messori complained, "If anyone is responsible for dechristianizing Italy, that person is Silvio Berlusconi. His networks are emblematic of a humanity for whom God is not even a conjecture."[5] But the religious allusions continued and became routine.

The opposition years (1995–2001) were "crossing the desert." Forza Italia supporters were invited "to become apostles of freedom" and "commit themselves to this mission" because "these are our values, this is our creed, this is our secular prayer." Candidates at the 2004 European elections were given the "Forza Italia Secular Creed," a selection of the leader's speeches, evangelically arranged into twelve readings. During the 2006 election campaign, Silvio confided, "I am the Jesus Christ of politics, a victim. I endure everything. I sacrifice myself for everyone."[6]

That irony was absent at the unveiling of the "party of love"[7] on December 26, 2009, and at the show put on in

Rome's Piazza San Giovanni three months later. The prime minister gathered the majority's candidates for regional governorships and announced, "I appoint you missionaries of truth and freedom to go forth and convince those who have yet to be convinced!" He told them to place their hands on their hearts and read together:

> *Before these people*
> *representing all moderates,*
> *in the name of freedom,*
> *I hereby solemnly swear*
> *to implement in my region*
> *in agreement with the Italian government*
> *all the points of the pact for Italy*
> *presented today*
> *by Prime Minister Silvio Berlusconi.*[8]

There were twelve candidates, and Silvio was center stage. Leonardo Da Vinci could have sued for copyright infringement. Of course, the Rome event wasn't a supper, and in any case it wasn't going to be the last one.

There's a new religion in Italy.

"You know, I rather doubt that people are worried. My fear is that our people, too, may look favorably on a strong, doubt-free, ethical judgment. We live in a society where the clever people are the ones who have made money, are successful, and can engage other people's attention. Some may think that those who become rich, enjoy a successful career, and so on are the lucky ones. These are the false criteria used for judgment. I'm afraid people might not be shocked. And I wouldn't like to think the Church was complicit."

The observation came from Carlo Ghidelli, archbishop of Lanciano and Ortona, and a biblical scholar of international repute, just after revelations emerged about the prime minister's unconventional lifestyle. *Famiglia Cristiana* magazine railed at "indefensible conduct" that overstepped the "threshold of decency," thundering that the Italian Church "cannot ignore the moral crisis."[9]

Obviously, the Church cannot turn a blind eye, yet neither does it seem able to react. Slipping standards aren't restricted to Italy. Elsewhere, however, religious morality is backed up by civil ethics. If a German minister were found to have money of dubious provenance socked away overseas, she wouldn't be chased out of office because she had sinned. She'd be thrown out for graft.

It's not that these mechanisms are rusty in Italy: They don't exist. The doors of the Italian conscience open only under pressure, and not always even then. Public opinion has always considered politics to be a distant planet following an orbit of its own. Many Catholics—tired, despondent, or destitute of options—suppress their indignation. Some take the opportunity to claim mitigating circumstances. If that is the example, what can you expect from the rest of us?

There's a practical religion in Italy, one that weighs pros against cons.

It refrains from poking its nose into the methods used in Libya to block migrants (a long way from Benedict XVI's "invitation to embrace legitimate human diversity"). It avoids examining too closely a fiscal federalism that could exacerbate the inequalities dividing northern Italy from the south.[10] Practical religion maintains that blasphemy has to be "contextualized"[11] and is prepared to shut both eyes to the carryings-on of a "whoremongering prime minister"— the jocular definition comes from the man himself[12]—if it gets what it considers right and proper from him.

Practical religion detaches rules from behavior. It claims it wants to help the humble while letting the big shots get on with it. When education minister Mariastella Gelmini wanted to show that the People of Freedom was the party most sensitive "to the defense and promotion of the individual and the family," she said, "It's no coincidence that it is led by a man like Silvio Berlusconi with a track record as a businessman in Christian Democrat Lombardy. A man who supported Catholic-inspired initiatives—I'm thinking of the San Raffaele hospital. A man who was educated by the Salesian Fathers."

Arts minister Sandro Bondi quoted Benedict XVI, pointing out that "a Christianity of charity without truth would be more or less interchangeable with a pool of good sentiments, helpful for social cohesion, but of little relevance." Bernhard Scholz, president of the Compagnia delle Opere, a galaxy of thirty-five thousand enterprises linked to Comunione e Liberazione, warned, "Consistent personal behavior, although important and desirable, is not the only criterion for judging the political actions of those who govern us. There is a more important issue: whether politics concedes freedom to operations working for the common good."[13]

Even Cardinal Angelo Scola, then patriarch of Venice, seemed to be trying to defuse Catholic indignation. "It is becoming necessary to free the category of witness from the burdensome encumbrance of moralism, which weighs it down, reducing it for the most part to the coherence of an ultimately self-referential subject."[14] His Eminence will forgive us, but that sounds like a way of putting conscience back in its box. Many Italians have already done so; others can't wait to join them.

There's a disoriented religion in Italy.

Congregations in the country's twenty-six thousand parishes are sincerely against abortion, honestly perplexed by euthanasia, and frankly opposed to joining two people of the same sex in marriage. Who do they vote for? There are more than one million divorced people in Italy, some of whom would like to approach the Eucharist. Watching the divorced and remarried Silvio B. receive communion at Raimondo Vianello's funeral,[15] they might have felt they could turn a blind eye to his unconventional relationships.

There is in Italy a majority that stiffens at the constant demands of the Muslim community. The Center-Left beats around this particular bush, while the Center-Right bristles. "Get off your high horse, comrades. Admit it. You want to see a Qaddafi-style performance right here, and not just for a couple of days, but on an ongoing basis, in every town in Italy. In the name of your sacred notion of a multi-ethnic, multi-cultural society, and the right of anyone to worship anywhere, you adore the idea of a mosque in every village in Italy, let alone at Ground Zero."[16] Nicholas Farrell in *Libero* newspaper. Simplistic? Obviously, but also effective.

Sociologist Giuseppe De Rita opines, "Catholics have an emerging ability to be postmodern, that is postindustrial, posturban, postmediatic, and postsecularized."[17] All quite probably true. But in the wake of Christian Democracy's demise, Catholics no longer have a political home. They seek shelter where they can. And Mr. B. is happy to buff up his Christianity-friendly image by providing some.

On *Porta a Porta*—the talk show where Mr. B. likes to open his book of revelations—he insisted on reading out loud the letter written by the archbishop of L'Aquila for the inauguration of a kindergarten rebuilt after the 2009 earthquake: "The Gospel condemns those who talk but fail to act, and Gospel praises those who shun idle chatter for concrete action."[18] A nod to doubting Catholics, or perhaps a self-serving bow. It depends on your point of view.

Italians have a gut feeling for the mystical, and Silvio has studied it. Italy also has hypocritical Catholics, lackadaisical

Catholics, and undecided Catholics. They tend to vote the same way.

The hypocrites, for whom religion is a matter of appearances, are glad they're not the only ones.

Lackadaisical Catholics are loud in defense of non-specific Christian values, and join the Northern League's Po Valley–based pagan chorus.

The waverers sigh, "I have reservations about the man, but the political program is more important."

"There is a world that uses religious principles as a veil to hide something else," wrote Father Michele Falabretti, head of the Youth Pastoral Team for the diocese of Bergamo. "It's a world that pretends to have forgotten that Christianity is a deep sharing of life, founded on the commandment of love, and demands strong commitment to others. A world of devout atheists that can still shut up anyone with just ten words: 'You're not going to vote for pro-abortion Communists, are you?' Berlusconi is successful because he offered the simplest, most immediate answer, one that lets a Catholic come out of the polling booth thinking, 'At least I didn't take any risks.'"[19]

Parish priests and bishops raised their eyes to the heavens when the notoriously promiscuous Mr. B. turned up at the 2009 Family Day demonstration. But as Ferruccio Pinotti and Udo Gümpel point out in *L'Unto del Signore* (*The Lord's Anointed*), "The Vatican seemed determined to exploit the Berlusconi government's conservative stance on issues such as abortion, divorce, assisted procreation, civil unions, and living wills."[20] Another thing for dioceses to take into account.

But is it good strategy to be happy with laws and compliments? This ally is turning into a competitor. For many Italians, he is the idol of an alien, hedonistic, secular faith. Monsignor Ghidelli suspects that today's Unholy Trinity is Money, Success, and Power, which puts Mr. B. in a leading position to be its prophet. He is not, as Gianni Baget Bozzo claimed, "Catholics' true moral leader,"[21] nor has he "raised the bar of ethics in politics" (hardly a Herculean task). No, he is "God's gift to Italy,"[22] as Father Verzé insisted under the spires of Milan cathedral.

We just need to know what God had in mind. Is Mr. B. manna from heaven, or a Job-style test of our faith?

CHAPTER THREE

The Robinson Factor

nough of this climate of excessive, Jacobin-style *legalism. I will prevent a return to a past that Italians no longer want.*[1]

He's not a necessity of history, or an inevitable consequence of the Italian national character. Mr. B. comes from an insight. His own. He understands solidarity with those who try, admiration for those who succeed, distrust for authority, indulgence for the accused, and the entirely Italian ability to squeeze into the space between lofty principles and low-minded interest.

Every Italian feels like Robinson Crusoe. The beach we have to survive on is a mysterious, inhospitable state with its

34

pointless laws, molasses-slow bureaucracy, and enterprise-choking taxes. Every now and again, we see Friday's footprints in the sand. Someone was here before us.

A rich, famous individualist doesn't have to explain the virtues of individualism. Since the early days of Forza Italia in 1993, he has nationalized the principles of the British Conservative Right so dear to Professor Giulio Urbani. It was Urbani who first put forward the idea of a party to counterbalance the Left when Christian Democracy and the Socialist Party crumbled. Margaret Thatcher's "Less State, More Market" turned into a no-holds-barred free-for-all on the journey from London to Milan.

Freedom to make, unmake, invoke, invent, ignore, sidestep, or interpret laws according to conscience and convenience. Buoyed by private success, Mr. B. has built on the mistrust of anything publicly owned, the irritation at rules, and the deep sense of satisfaction that derives from finding an individual solution to a shared problem.

In Italy, there is no real cohesive public pressure for a new, fairer, more efficient tax system. People evade the one they have. Although he denies it, Mr. B. said at a press conference on February 17, 2004, "If they want upward of 50 percent of my income in taxes, I feel that's an unfair demand. I feel morally authorized to evade as much as I can."[2] In the United States, this would be seditious; in Italy, it was merely stating the obvious, and a bit late at that.

Hyperregulated anomy—the absence of accepted rules with a superabundance of pointless ones—is the ocean on which Italy is adrift. Over the years, the country's response has been given various names—surviving, getting by, easing along—and has offered many unspoken invitations (come to an arrangement, sort it out yourself, the good Lord helps those who help themselves). But the good Lord got tired of having to deal with Italians.

So Berlusconi stepped in.

This looks more like an anthropological shift than a judicial emergency. Who are the ravenous new Italians who fill our newspapers nowadays? Where did they come from? There have always been corrupters and corruptees. Once, however, both were aware that they were different. There was a whiff of shame that helped to explain them, even if it did not absolve them.

Today, the corrupt are beyond explaining. These people preen. They smile and change the subject. They occupy local administrations, professional offices, health boards, seats in Parliament, jobs in government, university appointments, and public services. They can't wait to sell their souls for a sinecure or an apartment, encouraged by a sense of impunity. What makes them preen is not so much the wealth they accumulate—which often cannot be enjoyed for fear of discovery—as the feeling that they outsmarted the world. Any residual pangs of conscience are silenced by the conviction that everyone, or nearly everyone, does it.

Creating an army of accomplices, even when their guilt is trivial in comparison. Instilling a fear of being found out. Leveraging the sense of insecurity of a nation accustomed (or determined, or forced—pick your own adjective) to living with illegality. Recruiting all the landlords who never declared their rent income, and anyone who has mentioned accepting payment in cash on a taped or untaped phone call. Watch out. Tomorrow it could be you. Yes, substituting Buttoned Lips for the Clean Hands corruption investigations was a masterpiece of political plastic surgery.

A reader who signs himself Jimmy Vescovi asks, "Did you know they 'contract out' degree theses? I am a ghost writer for students with more than sixty theses to my credit, and in subjects that are not exactly related. 'To my credit' means I planned, wrote, and corrected them. I've also had inquiries from high-school students, but I turned them down. They asked me to use very simple language, and even make the odd mistake! Did you know that some parents give their kid a full package of three exams + degree thesis as a birthday present?"[3]

We could advise Jimmy V. to find a new job, unless he wants to be an accomplice to fraud (a degree is a legally valid qualification). However, we need to focus on the buyers. Getting a thesis written and then submitting it as your own is not just wrong; it's a crime. Paying for it is not merely improper; it's crazy. Just think about it. Loving parents take cash from the bank to buy someone else's work and give the kids' laziness a cuddle. What a magnificent lesson.

Many Italians have lost sight of how serious their actions are. They have stopped thinking "this is right" and "that's wrong." If they're caught, they're outraged (What? For such a little thing?). Bad examples from above can't explain it. If stuff like this goes on, it means that something is wrong with Italian society. Or perhaps it was never right.

In universities elsewhere in Europe, exam candidates who copy are pilloried. That's the deterrent. Students in American colleges take assessment tests home with them, promising on their honor to complete them without help. Over here, there are parents who buy their kid's degree thesis, and explain how to beat the bar examination or the entry test for med school. And if the little darlings are found out, they'll help them to appeal.

"It's wonderful to be Italian," sighs one character in Giovanni Arpino's soccer novel *Azzurro tenebra*. "Italians forgive others and themselves of all the vices. They understand. Italians invented mitigating circumstances."[4]

We are inventors, experts, and connoisseurs who specialize in finding justifications. Disappointments have made us suspicious, but that doesn't mean we can't have periodic bursts of revolutionary fervor. Like Mazzini and Mussolini, Mr. B. knows this instinctively. But whereas Giuseppe M. nobly dreamed of a new Italy, and Benito M. improbably attempted to build one, Silvio didn't bother trying. Almost from the outset, he realized that the only tolerable revolution for most Italians was one that revolutionized nothing at all.

Bill Emmott, long-serving editor in chief of *The Economist* (1993–2006) and author of *Forza, Italia*, a journey through the good and less good aspects of the Bel Paese, opines:

> The Bad Italy is not Italy at all, but it is certainly Italian. It is not Italy because it is all about selfishness. It starts of course with corruption and criminality, but is better described as the urge to seek power in order to abuse it for self-interested purposes, to amass power to reward friends, family, bag-carriers, and sexual partners regardless of merit or ability. . . . And I know all about the ambivalence deep in every Italian, the belief that laws should be enforced and obeyed, taxes paid, just not by me. Yet there is something extra about the Bad Italy. This sort of selfishness involves a special and even willfully destructive disregard for any wider community or, especially, national interests, institutions, laws, and values.[5]

Bending rules, piloting public employment competitions, finding shortcuts, and obtaining favors that go beyond courtesies all tend to be justified by the general public if they are to the benefit of their own group, family, association, trade, or profession. The "amoral familism" analyzed in the 1950s by American anthropologist Edward Banfield thrives and survives. "The inability of the villagers to act together for their common good"[6] is still an Italian characteristic.

Encouraged by the infrequency of reprimands and the absence of any consequences, society has simply renamed its vices. Now it calls them "the way we do things."

It's quite normal for Mr. B. to be proud of his children and take care of their future: Marina gets Mondadori, Piersilvio takes over Mediaset, A.C. Milan may go to Barbara, and he'll sort out the other two later. What is less normal is regarding his children as an excuse for ignoring his monumental conflict of interest:

"In explaining over the years why he has not sold off his media empire, he has frequently said: 'I can't, I have five children.' To foreign observers this seems a preposterous statement—a premier ignoring the general good of the nation for his own family's interests—but it sounds less odd to the millions of Italians who own their own business and whose primary obsession is passing it on to their children," notes Alexander Stille in his *The Sack of Rome*.[7]

Mr. B. has maintained since his entry into politics that his conflict of interest was resolved at the polls: "Italians know who I am and what I own, and they still vote for me."[8] From the legal viewpoint, this is less than accurate. In elections, Italians choose how to form a parliament, not forget about a problem. It doesn't stand up logically, either. We could ask ourselves just how free that consensus is, given that the conflict of interest concerns the media.

It is, however, true that Italy's ruling class has never bothered with the issue. Those active in politics didn't want rules that would shackle their business interests; and those engaged in business did not want rules that would cramp their political activities, Sergio Romano reminds us.[9] Public opinion seems equally indifferent. Apart from this, Italy has always sloshed around in a soup of conflicting interests.

We put up with councilors who have links with constructors; examiners who are colleagues of their examinees; tenured faculty related to tenure-seeking staff; doctors whose expenses are paid by Big Pharma; public works officials who give contracts to business partners; public school teachers who give private lessons to their students; and journalists who own press agencies. Why get worked up about a politician who owns the media that should be keeping tabs on him?

So, no change. We tolerate him and he justifies us.

Not even custom-tailored legislation provoked the outcry you would expect in a democracy. Sergio Romano again, in a *Corriere della Sera* editorial, calls it "a collection of laws (all subscribed and voted by Gianfranco Fini's followers as well) that had no other aim than to solve the problems of a single individual." Even as benevolent a commentator as Giuliano Ferrara has admitted, "It is clear that Berlusconi has never had any desire to put his anomalous status, which is also his identity, behind him."[10] Ferrara added, "It makes no sense to blame him for looking after his own affairs, defending himself from aggressive magistrates, and his assets from sentences that seek to break them up. . . . Silvio Berlusconi's business is the nation's business. Period."

The upshot is that for years Italians have watched a man use public powers to take care of his private business. We will draw a veil over the amnesties for tax evasion and building code violations, the abolition of inheritance tax, the new rules for supplementary pension schemes, and the soccer decree, from which Mr. B. benefited, although he wasn't the only one.

We will close both eyes to laws 350/2003 and 311/2004, which put government incentives in place for decoders in the run-up to digital TV, the main beneficiary of which was Solari.com, owned by Paolo Berlusconi. We will ignore decree-law 352/2003, which enabled Rete 4 to continue over-the-air analog broadcasting until 2010. We will disregard the Gasparri law 112/2004, which introduced the integrated communications system for calculating revenue, thus favoring Mediaset. We will pass over law 185/2008, which raised the rate of value added tax from 10 to 20 percent for Mediaset's main commercial rival, Sky Italia.[11] And we will ignore decree law 40/2010, which enabled Mondadori to pay the tax authorities €8.6 million in settlement of a case involving €173 million in unpaid taxes, which fines and interest had bloated to €350 million.[12]

But we haven't mentioned the law on letters rogatory (367/2001), which makes it more difficult to acquire evidence from abroad; or the decriminalization of false accounting (61/2001); or the Cirami law on legitimate suspicion as grounds for disqualifying a judge (248/2002); or the "Lodo

Schifani" decree on immunity for holders of the five highest offices of state (140/2003, subsequently pronounced unconstitutional by the supreme court's consultative committee in ruling 13/2004); the ex-Cirielli law (251/2005), which triggered time bars for the offenses of perverting judicial proceedings and false accounting in the Lodo Mondadori, Lentini, and Mediaset TV rights trials, in which Mr. B. was one of the defendants; the Lodo Alfano decree (124/2008), which suspended criminal proceedings against holders of the highest offices of state (before it was declared unconstitutional by ruling 262/2009, it enabled Mr. B. to extricate himself from the Mills trial, in which he was a defendant).

Finally in 2009 and 2010, the government majority attempted to introduce the so-called short trial. A fascinating name in the land of trials that never end. In what amounts to an amnesty in disguise,[13] a transitional provision would apply this law to trials currently underway. Including ones where Mr. B. is in the dock.

To take in just how inappropriate these laws are, you need to understand them, and if the public is going to understand them, someone has to provide an explanation. For that, you need airtime on TV. And obviously, there isn't much of it. Some are happy with the explanation offered by Mediaset chair Fedele Confalonieri, for whom his friend Silvio is always a victim of circumstance: "If there are *ad personam* [made-to-measure] laws, it's because there are *ad personam* sentences."[14]

Yet many Italians don't hear excuses.

They assume that those who can, do, and those who don't, can't.

"We were among the last to join the consortium of European nations, and we gave ourselves a modern organization at a faster, forced pace to achieve the level others had reached naturally, by inner-driven evolution," wrote Silvio Guarnieri in his *Carattere degli italiani*[15] (*The Character of the Italians*). Guarnieri was a curious figure, the son of a notary and a true-believing Communist from a Catholic family, he was a habitué of the Giubbe Rosse café in Florence and a friend of writers Carlo Emilio Gadda and Elio Vittorini.

This is a roundabout approach, of course, but if we don't start like this, we won't be able to explain the absence, or lukewarm nature, of some reactions. Italy has a tradition of bending the knee (the Medici Factor) while presenting itself effectively (the Truman Factor), and exploiting suspicion and self-sufficiency. It's Italy's Robinson Factor. This combination has produced the imagination that enchants the world, and the cynicism that puzzles it.

People abroad simply can't understand why we put up with such slow legal processes. A note from the European Council tells us that five and a half million civil actions are pending in Italian courts, along with more than three million criminal cases. The wait for a ruling in civil cases averages six years and ten months.[16] Judicial proceedings thus become Mr. B.'s natural allies, enabling him to pose as a genuine victim to a public of potential victims. ("There is a criminal association in the magistracy!"; "We'll push through law reform for citizens and honest judges.")[17] Some see the difference. Many sympathize. And many are more than some, as anyone in power well knows.

Mr. B., too, has in mind a national civic community in which citizens "regard the public domain as more than a battle-ground for pursuing personal interest,"[18] and he offers this vision to the electorate. Yet this is not the result of a project. It is more a by-product of the leader's dreams, an automatic process in which no one is asked to make any sacrifices for mutual advantage.

Plenty of Italians get busy for the common good, of course. Voluntary organizations straddle the political divide. Movements and associations attract people of every ideological hue. Some don't vote for Berlusconi, but accept his tacit invitations to take individualism to extremes; others vote for him believing that since he has few ideals, he is the perfect leader for those who have many.

Mr. B. doesn't preach, prompt, or pronounce. He lives and lets live. The problem is that, what with all the suspicions and court proceedings, he doesn't live terribly well, and we could live better.

CHAPTER FOUR

The Truman Factor

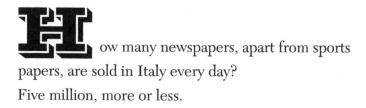 ow many newspapers, apart from sports papers, are sold in Italy every day?
Five million, more or less.

How many Italians regularly use bookstores?
Five million, more or less.

How many watch Sky TG24 and TG La7 news?
Five million, more or less.

How many watch early-evening current affairs TV programs *Annozero* and *Ballarò*?
Five million, more or less.

How many watch news analysis programs on late-evening TV?
Five million, more or less.

How many Italians browse major news websites?
Five million, more or less.

How many surf the Net from their smartphone/cellphone/
handheld device?
Five million, more or less.

How many buy stuff on the Internet?
You got it: five million, more or less.[1]

You get the feeling they're always the same five million
people. We'll call them the Five Million Club, since many
of the members claim to speak English. Is it important? Yes,
but less than you might think. Is it decisive? Well, it decides
the tone and direction of national debate, but it doesn't
decide elections.

The Club includes government supporters and opponents, free thinkers and rent-a-thinkers, liberals, libertar-
ians, and—rather a lot of—libertines. The intellectual Left
adores the Five Million Club, splashing around in it like a
puppy in a creek. The campaigning Right and the government also enjoy the Club, but unlike their opponents, they
know that political destinies are decided elsewhere. On
television, for example. On free-to-air television from seven
P.M. to nine P.M., to be precise.

The evening ritual of watching the TV news, even in these days of digital TV and fast-multiplying channels, attracts almost twenty million viewers. Its impact is on the wane, of course,[2] but we're still talking about almost two-fifths of the adult population, enough to make any politician's mouth water. Say you want to highlight crime when your opponents are in power, or play it down when you're back in power. The evening news is the place to do it.

This has actually happened. Figures to hand, Michele Polo writes in *Notizie S.p.A.*(*News, Inc.*), "The intensity of crime-related news stayed at the baseline level during the 2006 election campaign, when the Center-Right was in power, whereas it underwent strong dramatization, led by Mediaset group news programs, after the Center-Left took office. There was a subsequent slackening of media attention after the Center-Right won at the polls again in 2008."[3]

And who's in charge of the Center-Right? Who has owned almost all of private television since the 1980s, and today controls most of publicly owned television as the head of government? Who publishes major periodicals and could soon also be in charge of the leading dailies?[4] Step forward Mr. B., for whom all of this is not a problem. "I will never sell my television channels" and "conflict of interest? I am the best guarantee,"[5] he said on April 1 and 18, 1994, having just moved into the prime minister's Palazzo Chigi offices. Since then, he has made hundreds of statements, comments, reassurances, and promises on the issue. But he has not actually done anything about it. He's not selling and claims there is no problem.

Non-Italians who live in democracies, regardless of where they are or what politics they profess, are surprised. British historian David Gilmour writes in *The Pursuit of Italy* (Penguin, 2011):

> Yet more invidious . . . has been the power of a single individual, a politician in a democracy, to command almost the entire output of the most important sector of his nation's media. Berlusconi regarded the notion of an independent broadcasting corporation as simply ludicrous. After becoming prime minister in 1994, he declared it would be "anomalous" for a country to have a state television that did not support the government elected by the people.[6]

Mr. B. talks about "good journalism" (television) and "bad journalism" (the papers).[7] But then he attacks programs like *Annozero*, which, according to one minister, "cost us six hundred thousand votes in the last election."[8] Like previous tenants of Palazzo Chigi, the current prime minister views the state RAI television as spoils of war and, as we have seen, he is unperturbed by the fact that he owns three private networks. What is harder to understand is why most Italians are equally unperturbed.

❖

We don't live in the *The Truman Show*. We are not a nation of Jim Carreys, unaware of what is going on. Let's just say that someone is doing the directing, and it isn't Peter Weir.[9]

TG4 news and *Studio Aperto* flaunt their support for their owner and our head of government, happy that it's the same person, but other persuasion mechanisms are more subtle.

All it took was for Enrico Mentana and TG La7 news to introduce standard images for all politicians in summer 2010 and the leader of the opposition, Pier Luigi Bersani, stopped looking as if he was glistening with sweat, cowering before the microphones, and incapable of forming a complete sentence. In contrast, without the flattering shots from below, the prime minister suddenly looked shorter and less slim.

Needless to say, you can lose an election even if you control television. Silvio has managed that twice, in 1996 and 2006. But without that control, he might have lost more often, or more heavily.

By sweeping corruption under the carpet, hiding embarrassments, and hushing up problems and wrongdoing, television is important for the news it doesn't broadcast, the questions it doesn't ask, the criticisms it doesn't make, the scandals it doesn't expose, and for the personalities it creates, keeps in the public eye, destroys, or forgets.

If things were any different, there would be no sense to Vladimir Putin's clampdown on Russian television, Nicolas Sarkozy's attention to French broadcasting, Tony

Blair's spats with the BBC, or the behavior of American politicians. As Al Gore reminds us,[10] U.S. politicos buy up millions of dollars of air space on TV networks in the knowledge that thirty seconds in the right time slot can make all the difference.

Television matters in a democracy. Anyone who denies this, and claims that it plays no part in shaping consensus, is being cute, or naive. A Censis statistics institute study (*Elezioni 2009: come si sono informati gli italiani* [*2009 Elections—How Italians Got Their Information*]) reveals that during the campaign for the European elections, 69.3% of voters acquired information for their voting decisions through news and comments on TV newscasts. TV news is the main medium for guiding voting decisions, especially with the less well educated, among whom the figure rises to 76%, pensioners (78.7%), and homemakers (74.1%).

You need to talk about this on television to alert society's conscience, but it is simply not possible. Television's controllers don't like people talking about television on television. And even if it were possible, we have to admit that society's conscience is in poor condition.

Silvio Berlusconi was born in the Isola district of Milan on September 29, the same day as Democratic Party leader Pier Luigi Bersani. The Center-Right's Mr. B. is not from outer space, as his opponents like to imply to cover up their own inadequacies (when the Center-Left was in power, it failed to pass a law to regulate conflicts of interest and free the RAI state broadcaster from party interference). As we have attempted to explain, Mr. B. picks up, amplifies, and forgives widely shared attitudes. In Italy, the idea that newspapers and television should be independent is looked on as naive, self-deluding, or hypocritical. We don't like to seem naive or deluded. Hypocritical, we can talk about.

Most Italians do not believe that the media are a check that democracy needs. If a latter-day Thomas Jefferson were to land at Naples or Palermo and say again, "Were it left to me to decide whether we should have a government without newspapers, or newspapers without a government, I should not hesitate a moment to prefer the latter," the locals would tell him they'd happily give up both if someone would take away the trash. In Milan or Rome, they'd want to replace H.L. Mencken's lamppost ("Journalism is to politician as dog is to lamppost."[11]) with a bone. A tail-wagging dog is more likely to get a bone.

Silvio just reads, with fewer scruples and more competence, from a script we already know: The government controls television, leaving the opposition with one or two token shows. The possibility that, in the case of a victory for the Right, ownership of private television might be compounded by control of public broadcasting proved too challenging a concept for the Left, let alone ordinary Italians with home loans to pay off.

Yet the media are gaining popularity everywhere as weapons in the political struggle. It is the brilliant,

GOP-supporting Fox News that is making headway in America, not the classic CNN. Only the BBC, the *Financial Times*, and *The Economist* appear not to have any a priori enemies in the UK. In Italy, we don't even have to break with tradition. Sticking up for our side against an adversary is, as we shall see, a concept we know and relish.

In this respect, Mr. B.'s admirers resemble his detractors: both seek reassurance for their beliefs. It holds true for the papers, as it does for television news. The general public doesn't want doubts with its cappuccino or evening meal. Critical sense pays the price of Italy's recent acquaintance with democracy and long-standing partisan spirit. The masses, like the audience in *The Truman Show*, don't want objections: They want reassurance. They're not looking for problems: They want a plot. They want entertainment, not information. Without realizing that this time, they are not watching. They're taking part.

Thirty-year-old Truman Burbank, star of *The Truman Show*, doesn't know that since he was born, he has been living in a colossal reality show, broadcast live to millions of spectators. Seahaven, the pretty little town where he lives, is one huge television studio. His friends and acquaintances are actors, while the production company controls everything and everyone: meetings, friendships, love affairs, work, problems, and leisure time.

Seahaven is actually called Seaside. It's in Florida on the Gulf of Mexico, halfway between Fort Walton Beach and Panama City. This idyllic spot with its pale blue homes and white boardwalks is a real estate fantasy that sprang from the imagination of Robert Davis, who built it in 1979 to the canons of New Urbanism on land he inherited from his grandfather, re-creating the memories of his child-hood. The motto of the town, now the domain of wealthy American vacationers, is vaguely Orwellian: "More than a way of life, a way of living!" The fact that it was a film set is not publicized. Truman Burbank/Jim Carrey's house is in real life the home of a family whose members smile at inquisitive visitors, but make it clear that they do not feel flattered by the curiosity and would happily do without such visits.

What is so Trumanesque in Italy today? Well, the attempt to convince us that all is for the best in the best of all possible worlds, for a start. "There are two kinds of reality," Mr. B. has said. "The real one that ordinary people experience, and the reality that the papers describe, which is not real. It's pure fantasy."[12] Some might object that governments everywhere do that. True. But the Italian production is more insidious. This director knows what he's doing.

Mr. B. is not a dictator. His methods are not those of a dictatorship. He dreams of a pastel-tinted Italy and paints one in black and white to achieve it. Mr. B. wants an Italy of happy families and obedient children, busy towns, thriving companies, fast transport, and efficient services. In other words, he wants the country described in *Meno male che Silvio c'è* [*Thank Goodness for Silvio*].[13] Impossible, without collective sacrifice, but asking for sacrifice can wait. The asker might not be too popular.

"Silvio Berlusconi has managed to cast a spell over Italians for the last fifteen years with his words, slogans, jokes, anecdotes, and pledges, mesmerizing them with media therapy and preaching all-round optimism, confidence, and hope for a better future. So far, the majority has believed him the way you believe a prophet, a guru, or an oracle," writes Giovanni Valentini.[14]

Demagoguery? Is this a man who "talks to gratify his listeners, and holds them in the palm of his hand by playing to their worst prejudices and worst passions"?[15] Not precisely. A demagogue is an orator and, as we have seen, Silvio is a director. He creates the sets through which his characters move. Theoretically, they are free to improvise, but in practice they are acting out a screenplay written into their daily routine.

If the screenplay turns out to be less flexible than the cast, that's no problem. Change the screenplay. Mr. B.'s media constantly busy themselves with the projection of an image of optimism, efficiency, and competence. In a link-up with a correspondent at the L'Aquila G8 meeting, TG4 news was never going to inquire how much it cost to move the summit from La Maddelena. Instead, the question was "Two miracles have been accomplished: the Naples garbage crisis and this G8. What will the third miracle be?"[16]

The politician defends himself with the armor of a businessman, and the entrepreneur uses the weapons of politics. As it was in the beginning, is now, and ever shall be.

In 1995, a referendum proposed a maximum of one network per private owner, a ban on commercial breaks during films, and a cap on advertising revenue. The reaction was swift and terrible.

Mike Bongiorno, Fiorello, Gerry Scotti, Alberto Castagna, Valeria Marini, Marco Columbro, Lorella Cuccarini, and Ezio Greggio were followed by Enrico Mentana, Antonio Di Pietro, the bombing of Baghdad during the Gulf War, John Paul II, Rabin and Arafat shaking hands, tanks in Tiananmen Square, clips from movies and TV shows, *Ghost*, *Twin Peaks*, *Dallas*, *The Thorn Birds*, and *The Lady in Red,* to a soundtrack featuring Louis Armstrong. Then the music and images disappeared. The screen went black for a few seconds. A message appeared: "1980–1995. For the past fifteen years of your life, you have had something extra. Canale 5, Italia 1, Rete 4. Let us be there for you. Choice is better." This is the ninety-second promo—conceived by Giorgio Gori and Davide Rampello at the behest of Fedele Confalonieri—that Fininvest launched yesterday at 6:05 P.M. on Canale 5 and that will also air over the next few days on the other channels.[17]

Nine years later, in 2004, Christian Democrat UDC leader Marco Follini, riding the wave of a good showing in the administrative elections, dared to defend the equal media access that Silvio Berlusconi detests. This is how talk show host Bruno Vespa describes the scene:

> FOLLINI: . . . I am amazed to see that you, Silvio, put equal media access at the top of the list.
>
> BERLUSCONI: It's a crucial issue, because it cost me four points in the election. You, Marco, are everywhere on RAI channels. You can't be so selfish you would stop other parties from paying for their own campaign commercials.
>
> FOLLINI: It's true that I am on RAI TV, and just as well. Bear in mind that I was on Mediaset TV news programs for all of forty-two seconds in the months of January and February 2004.
>
> BERLUSCONI: At least Mediaset doesn't attack you.
>
> FOLLINI: I'd like to see that.
>
> BERLUSCONI: Keep on like this and you will.[18]

Since then, Marco Follini has practically disappeared from Italian screens, along with other individuals who popped up on the Center-Right on one pretext or another and then turned out not to be welcome, such as referendum promoter Mario Segni, former ministers Rocco Buttiglione and Beppe Pisanu, Antonio Martino, Paolo Guzzanti, and Bruno Tabacci.

In 2009, having publicly condemned the visits of prostitutes (officially known as "escorts") to Berlusconi's Palazzo Grazioli residence in Rome, the editor in chief of the Catholic paper *Avvenire* was attacked by Vittorio Feltri's Berlusconi family-owned *Il Giornale* and forced to resign. One headline: "Supercensor Boffo Convicted of Harassment."[19]

In 2010, the flagship edition of Augusto Minzolini's TG1 news reported an almost two-month-long inquiry by the same paper into a party-owned apartment that was leased to the brother of Elisabetta Tulliani, partner of the leader of the Chamber of Deputies, Gianfranco Fini, who had been expelled from the People of Freedom. It's surprising that as experienced a treader of the political boards as Fini couldn't hear the casting director's voice offstage saying, "Next, please."

The director makes the decisions, but Truman doesn't know.

Why doesn't this use of the media have voters up in arms? Well, few people ask themselves whether it is normal for anyone who criticizes the government to be pilloried on media controlled by the head of government. It could be because in the past, the Italian press had no compunction about waging campaigns on behalf of the boss of the day. The Communist Party always used *L'Unità* newspaper as a tool of political struggle. The Right did the same with *Secolo d'Italia*. There is a difference, though. Those papers were destroyers, while Mr. B. has a whole fleet of aircraft carriers, battleships, and torpedo-toting submarines.

There's no need to monitor every television program: The controllees control themselves. When Silvan the magician good-naturedly offered to "lend Berlusconi his magic wand" to tackle the post-earthquake reconstruction in Abruzzo, the alarmed presenter of the Sunday afternoon *Domenica In* program Lorena Bianchetti blustered, "I wanted to say something . . . because your remark was absolutely personal . . . whereas I want to take this opportunity to thank the institutions that have been truly present on the ground . . ."[20]

On a late-night news program, with only the Five Million Club watching, this would not have happened. On a lowbrow afternoon show, it did.

Italians demand miracles from those who govern them: It's one way of avoiding effort, sacrifice, and admissions. That's why over the past ninety years, we have been Fascists without meaning it, anti-Fascists without believing in it, Christian Democrats without admitting it, Socialists without putting our faith in it, referendum supporters without understanding it, and Berlusconians without realizing it.

Mr. B. loves being thought of as the miracle worker, a reputation he is prepared to share with Someone Else. He, too, offers the Promised Land, which is always just over the horizon. Out of reach, it cannot therefore disappoint. And to stage this show, the prophet has to be screenwriter, set designer, and cinematographer, as well as director. There are spotlights to turn off and background lighting to adjust if you want to convince the general public that a beautiful new day is always dawning.

Why talk about organized crime, if it upsets people? Just because the minister of the interior, the magistrates, and the police have enjoyed success in this area? "If I find the people who made nine series of *La Piovra* and the ones who write books about the Mafia and go around the world giving Italy such a great reputation, I swear I'll throttle them!"[21] said Mr. B., mentioning "literature, the cultural framework, *Gomorra*." You might object that Silvio's publishing house, Mondadori, printed Roberto Saviano's book *Gomorra*, and Silvio's television, Canale 5, broadcast that series on the boss of bosses, Totò Riina. But Silvio's rhetoric is not logical; it's emotional, like that of many Italians.

"When you flick through the papers in the morning, they foster fears that are beyond reason and beyond reality!" he complained at a Palazzo Chigi media briefing. He ended with an invitation: "We have to encourage press, publishers, and editors not to spread panic or fuel fears. Hence my invitation to the business community. Make your impact on the media more effective. Threaten not to place your advertising in media that are themselves factors in the crisis."[22]

For the Five Million Club, it was a clumsy invitation. For everyone else, an understandable reaction.

CHAPTER FIVE

The Hoover Factor

Mr. B. may know how to sell, but plenty wanted to buy.

He couldn't have found buyers for his political wares if the nation hadn't been on a shopping spree. Why? We've seen some of the reasons and will see others later: empathy, new influences, ancient habits, and a lack of alternatives. In the early 1990s, Italians were "tired of delays and thirsty for effectiveness,"[1] Barbara Spinelli has noted. It's a pity that we settled for the political equivalent of our usual cappuccino at the bar.

Still, the man knows how to sell. In fact, he's as good as the Hoover salesmen who set out to win over the United

States in the 1920s. In Canton, Ohio, sixty-year-old asthmatic and dust allergy sufferer James M. Spangler invented a suction sweeper using the blades of a fan, the motor from a sewing machine, a wooden box, a pillowcase, and a brush handle. Spangler had no money for investment, so in 1908 he sold the patent to a cousin's husband, William "Boss" Hoover, who started selling it door-to-door with a ten-day free trial.

> *There's nothing like a Hoover®*
> *When you're dealing with dirt!*

Back in the 1950s, Mr. B. paid his way through college by selling electric brushes, taking photographs at weddings and funerals as a sideline.[2] He worked out Italy's allergies and many years later introduced his own version of *Porta a Porta,* literally *Door to Door,* which by then had become a television talk show. The trial period is no longer free and it's lasted seventeen years.

Mr. B. is adept at making over the packaging without changing the product. Here are his classics.

THE NEW MAN

In 1994, Mr. B. presented himself as standing apart from the party system, a businessman on loan to politics. Forza Italia voters, a demographic that included many homemakers (21.8%) and not very many college graduates (3.8%), did not know about the meetings with Socialist leader Bettino Craxi and Christian Democrats, or about Fininvest's 3.5 billion lire debt, which prompted Giuliano Urbani, the man who inspired Mr. B.'s entry into politics at an Arcore meeting on June 29, 1993, to say, "In the beginning, I could see Berlusconi had mixed feelings, which were eighty percent fear."[3] If they had known, those voters wouldn't have thought it important. The electoral battle between a Milanese businessman noted for his colorful television channels (Silvio Berlusconi) and a career politician from Turin noted for his gray mustache (Achille Occhetto) was a foregone conclusion.

Polish up a pre-used item and it looks newer than new. Mr. B. continues, convincingly, to pose as an outsider. Phoning from Moscow to a People of Freedom training session at Gubbio on September 11, 2010, Silvio said Italy would not have a lame duck government, a government crisis "would be criminal," and "old-school wheeler-dealer politics" would not win the day.[4] The fact that he had been head of government for eight years, and of the opposition for the same length of time, changed nothing. His opponents were the old-school wheeler-dealers; he was the exciting new option.

THE PRACTICAL MAN

Silvio's January 26, 1994 video announcing his entry into politics is known, papal encyclical-style, by its first few words: *L'Italia è il paese che amo* (Italy is the country I love).

From then to the Contract with the Italians presented on television on May 8, 2001, five days before the vote that marked his comeback, and the proclamation of the "can-do government that tackles and solves emergencies old and new" from the podium in Rome's Piazza San Giovanni on March 20, 2010,[5] the method at critical moments has never varied. OSE: Omit, Simplify, Enlarge. Customers think they understand, get enthusiastic, and buy.

In his 2001 Contract, inspired by Republican Newt Gingrich's 1994 Contract with America, Mr. B. pledged to:

- reduce tax pressure

- introduce local foot patrol officers and cut crime

- raise minimum pensions

- start new public works

- cut unemployment in half

He promised not to stand again at the next election unless he fulfilled four of the five promises. As we know, fiscal pressure remained unchanged, unemployment failed to drop by half, and public works have produced more graft than new roads. But the customer will forget, if the salesman is good.

Mr. B.'s reputation as a can-do man has spread outside Italy. In his memoir *A Journey*, the former British prime minister, man of business, and man of the world Tony Blair, reveals how London secured the 2012 Olympics.

"There was one final person without whom we may not have won: Silvio Berlusconi. The previous August I had gone to visit him at his home in Sardinia to seek his help with the bid. Italy was a key player. He asked me how much it mattered to get the Olympics. 'It matters,' I said.

'Greatly?' he asked.

'Greatly,' I said. He said, 'You are my friend. I promise nothing but I see if I can help.' Typical Silvio, which is why I like him. Most politicians say 'I promise' but then do nothing. He said, 'I promise nothing,' but then delivered."[6]

Music to Mr. B.'s ears. And he has plenty of musicians to play it in public.

THE SUCCESSFUL MAN

The A.C. Milan soccer team is a metaphor for Mr. B.'s world. More than anything else, the Rossoneri, as they are known, combine his passion, vision, calculation, and interest.

In the wake of A.C. Milan's triumphs of the 1990s, which mirrored and facilitated his political success, and the two European wins in 2003 and 2007, Mr. B. seems to have fallen out of love with the team. A.C. Milan is perfect as it is, he cooed, leaving the glory and victories to rivals Inter Milan, which in the four seasons from 2007 to 2010 accumulated an advantage of seventy-nine championship points, even pulling off a historic hat trick of league championship,

Italian cup, and Champions League. Then one summer, out of the blue, Mr. B. bought two outstanding and very expensive players, Ibrahimovic and Robinho, in just forty-eight hours.

What was going on? According to *Il Giornale*'s sports correspondent Franco Ordine, it was a reaction to the "venom, the betrayals, and the disappointments that chairman Silvio Berlusconi had to put up with in politics." According to pollster Luigi Crespi, once Mr. B.'s blue-eyed boy, a "cross-sector lobby of business executives, politicians, journalists, entertainers, and A.C. Milan sympathizers" commissioned a survey with surprising results: "The prime minister risked losing 20 to 25 percent of A.C. Milan–supporting PDL voters. In electoral terms, this would have represented at least half a million votes, or two percentage points."[7]

An empty trophy cupboard is both a risk and a mark of shame. After a particularly embarrassing defeat against the newly promoted Cesena team, Mr. B. eschewed commenting on the indifferent debut of the above-mentioned Zlatan Ibrahimovic—who cost more than the entire Cesena squad—protesting: "The problem is that A.C. Milan often comes up against left-wing referees."[8] Replace "A.C. Milan" with "party," and "referees" with "magistrates," and it's clear the analysis is not new.

A conflict of interest? Not anymore. The prime minister's interests—national, international, private, family, social, sentimental, sexual, professional, sporting, televisual, advertising, financial, industrial, commercial, and political—are no longer in conflict. They are majestically intermingled, like the waters of a great river, and all point in the same direction. What about public opinion? It goes with the flow. And the opposition? Swept away by the flood every time.

If you Google the phrase "How to sell a product," you get 434 million hits. The top-ranked site is http://www.wikihow.com/Sell-a-Product. Its twelve tips show just how fantastic a salesman Mr. B. is. As for how good the product is, make up your own mind.

1. As well as getting good product information to the right people, it is important to translate the product's features into benefits for the customer, thus making it easier for them to buy.

Mr. B. managed to persuade many Italians that having him in government was in their interest. Some might object that all politicians do that. They do, of course, but there are politicians who do it better, faster, and with more imagination. Silvio's motto hasn't changed since he was selling homes and advertising: "You have to curve out with people who curve in, and curve in with people who curve out." He's not about to discuss tax evasion with an audience of potential evaders—so he's never going to broach the subject in Italy—but he doesn't miss an opportunity to chastise the slow approval of licenses and the complexity of the country's red tape.

2. During your presentation, confirm that your prospective buyer will want or need your product.

As we shall see, Mr. B. did not study at the Sorbonne, but he has attended business conventions, which are every bit as educational. His construction company, Edilnord, taught him the art of persuasion, optimism in the face of challenges, and the importance of the group. Advertising agency Publitalia imbued him with an awareness of the commercial value of standardization, the fatal attraction of repetition, and the techniques of ephemeral endearment, including memento gifts.

Eight world leaders are much easier to seduce than eight hundred young hopefuls who have to sell advertising space on commission. Silvio knows the rituals of the coffee break and the group photo. If Obama has posed a thousand times, then Mr. B. has done so a hundred times more. He knows when to pop up, how to smile, and what to say to grab the limelight, as he confirmed in 2009 when he told CNN's Paula Newton, "I bring good humor and optimism to the group. Having taught groups of people—sales teams and so on—so many times, in so many situations, that I know how to take the edge off serious speeches with one or two lighter moments."[9]

The Queen might get irritated, but she's not the one he has to win over.

3. Most successful products and services are bought, not sold. They are bought by people who have a need, and believe that the product will satisfy that need. This is often the result of marketing rather than selling, however.

Mr. B. loves irony and is no stranger to sarcasm. In contrast, he makes little use of understatement. For the man, that may be a limitation, but not for the salesman. Customers want him to be euphoric and innocent of doubt. This is how Mr. B. assessed his own performance in September 2009:

> I feel I am better than any other prime minister in the sixty-year history of the Italian republic. De Gasperi? He is a father of the fatherland and had a challenging task in foreign policy, but as far as domestic affairs are concerned, there is absolutely no comparison between what my government has done and what De Gasperi did.[10]

Historians will smile, but the message got through: "I say I am the best; it's up to you to prove the contrary." During the 1980s, he told his collaborators:

You must be jackhammers. Don't ask too much from people's intelligence. Be straightforward and persuasive. Repeat information; explain it simply. The simplest truths are the most difficult to forget.[11]

Only an American marketing guru could have put it better. No Italian politician could pass the buck for the country's financial woes to his predecessors as skillfully as this:

The governments from 1980 to 1992, with the external support of the Communist Party, voted 92 percent of the laws that have overburdened the national accounts, multiplying the national debt eightfold so that today we have the third highest public debt in the world.[12]

Did Silvio perhaps want to blame his friend Bettino Craxi, who was one of the leading politicians of the period? Obviously not. Live on television, he built a protective barrier around his Socialist patron, condemned the hated Communists, and found an excuse for the black hole of public finances. In fifty words. Not bad.

4. Selling the product rather than just offering it for sale almost always involves an emotional component.

Many American servicemen returning from the front at the end of the First World War were recruited into the army of Hoover reps. The work wasn't easy: long days, low earnings, and doors slammed in your face. The company started gratifying its best salesmen with medals, to which it gave military names, such as the DSM (Distinguished Service Medal), or titles such as Marksman. It was modest recognition that brought considerable gratification.

As Silvio realized. In 2006, Mr. B. distributed a kit to his "Blue Legionaries" ("180,000 individuals who believe in an ideal, know the project, persuade voters, defend our vote, and agree with Silvio Berlusconi and Forza Italia"). Legionaries? Mr. B. knows the gaps in Italy's memory. It doesn't bother him to use an ancient Roman term that Fascism plundered before he did. In August 2010, he ignored the Fascist connotations and announced the formation of "freedom squads" to carry out door-to-door canvassing, and then to monitor the vote. He must have had some vague suspicions, though, because the "squads" soon became "teams" ("I want 61,000 Freedom Teams in the 61,000 electoral districts").[13]

Personality cult, organization, and team spirit. It works. His opponents fail to see the attraction of badges, pins, and roles—for voters or candidates. Give an Italian a title, a rank, and a uniform, and you have a happy camper. We are a nation of puffed-up bosses, hopeful seconds-in-command, and organizational pyramids that look intimidating but actually reassure. They fill our lives, giving meaning to long waits and trivial tasks. One Italian in four is president of something or other; the other three hope to take over soon.

Silvio knows these mechanisms and turns them to his advantage. Aren't members of Parliament "representatives?" Well, they can grab a bag.

Just before the 1994 election, Mr. B. supplied candidates with two green canvas, faux leather–finished bags (one shoulder bag, one pilot style), which they paid for, containing:

- three red-, white-, and green-striped regimental ties with the Forza Italia slogan in the center;

- three large Tricolore flags with the same slogan;

- ten triangular gold-trimmed pennants;

- a set of pens with FORZA ITALIA in gold lettering;

- Fifteen videocassettes illustrating the points of the program, edited by Antonio Martino, of the LUISS University in Rome, and Gianni Marongiu, of the University of Genoa;

- two videocassettes, two compact discs, and three stereo cassettes with a karaoke version of the party anthem;

- stickers and badges in a range of formats;

- round badges with the leader's portrait;

- a brochure of the Fininvest empire, opening with the

group's symbol (a sculpture by Piero Cascella), a photo of the founder, and an illustrated list of assets in Italy and abroad;

- the *Declaration of Dr. Silvio Berlusconi on 1/26/1994—For My Country*.

There were guffaws from the Left when they heard about it. The Left duly lost, and the guffaws died away.

Fourteen years later, on the eve of the 2008 general election, tactics and tools were unchanged. Candidates were given kits—they didn't have to buy them this time—containing lapel pins, magnets, flag, the Charter of Values, the Seven Missions for the Future, the party manifesto, the Center-Left prime minister's sixty-seven new taxes listed one by one, and a book with forty pages of suggestions for debates and rallies ("Tools for Candidate Action"). One suggestion is to compare opponent Walter Veltroni to Joseph Stalin. Like this: "Even though he didn't have Adobe Photoshop, Stalin managed to airbrush Karl Radek out of a famous photograph of Kremlin leaders. But Radek's hands were still there and the photo was a political disaster. The same goes for Veltroni, the apprentice Stalin. He hides in Romano Prodi's wardrobe, but his hands, like those of Visco and Padoa-Schioppa, are visible in the excessive taxes that Italians are paying."[14]

There were more guffaws from the Left when they heard about it. Then the Left duly lost again, and again the guffaws died away.

5. Give your potential buyers many possible places to find out more about your information, including in the following ways: Person to person, by representatives, dealers, salesmen, radio, TV, word-of-mouth by customers, mail and email (in various forms), distribution at trade shows, seminars, telephone, fax, computer networks, product packaging, airline magazines, retail storefronts, space ads, and Internet.

The liturgy of the word is crucial to the Berlusconi rite. Selling a product—whether it's a suction sweeper or a political party—demands good speaking abilities. Mr. B. is an expert manipulator of monologues and monosyllables. He is less inclined to debate, since he cannot tolerate anyone contradicting him. If that happens, he slows, darkens, and dulls. He senses he is no longer loved, and stops trying to sell.

He writes with the clarity of a copywriter who cannot afford to be misunderstood. But Mr. B. excels at the spoken word, and it is on this that he has built his fortune. The risk is going too far. On television, he is extremely difficult to interrupt—few try, in any case—and he is convinced that his verbal flow of 6.5 syllables per second makes him mesmerizing.

We will discuss his vocabulary, which he can mold to suit his interlocutor, later on (The Zelig Factor). However, it is in syntax that Mr. B. has introduced his greatest innovations. Italian politics used to pride itself on the obscurity of its diction, which it regarded as a mark of distinction.

For decades, the implicit subordinate clause was the politician's trademark. Mr. B. introduced subject-verb-complement, and a single subordinate after the main clause. His customers/voters couldn't believe their ears: Entranced by the comprehensible form, they overlooked the unrealizable content.

> 6. The product information should be informative, true, and complete. Ideally, it should give the prospect all the information they need to buy on the spot.

Mr. B. loves to reel off figures, data, statistics, and percentages, for he knows how persuasive they are. Rarely is a listener able to refute him on the spot. Every so often, he gets it wrong. On one occasion, despite the gentle objections of interviewer Bruno Vespa, he insisted that "60 billion old lire" were "30 billion of today's euros."[15] Still, that's not the sort of stumble that's going to stop this marathon runner.

His advice to his members of Parliament, executives, and supporters is to use figures as often as possible. Government information publications are packed with figures: the booklet *5 anni di lavoro per l'Italia* (Five Years Working for Italy), distributed before the 2006 elections, has more numbers than a phone book. A scientific approach in an impressionistic nation. It's one more way of standing out and selling.

When necessary, this passion can entail a little distortion.

"In absolute terms, [I am] the man most persecuted by magistrates of all time, in the entire history of humanity anywhere in the world. [I have been] subjected to 106 trials, in all of which I was acquitted and two were time-barred," he complained on October 9, 2009. The actual number of trials is much lower. The following day, his daughter Marina put things in perspective in an interview with the *Corriere della Sera*. "What with trials and investigations, my father has been involved in court proceedings twenty-six times." Giuseppe D'Avanzo claims in *La Repubblica* that Silvio has been in the dock sixteen times and that, in the twelve trials which have now ended, only in three cases has he been acquitted (once fully).[16] In two trials, the act was no longer considered unlawful; in two more, amnesties extinguished the offenses; and in the other five cases, the defendant was granted mitigating circumstances, on three occasions benefitting from the halving of the statute of limitations passed by his own governing majority.

7. When selling a product one-on-one to a prospect, translating the information to benefits is even more important than the information required.

Umberto Eco writes:

What is striking—and, sadly, entertaining—about Berlusconi is his sales overkill. We don't need to invoke the ghost of Vanna Marchi, who was a caricature of pressure selling. Let's take a car salesperson.

The vendor starts off by saying you are buying a speed machine. Brush the accelerator pedal and you'll be doing a hundred. It's built for sports drivers. But as soon as you clear up that you've got five kids and an invalid mother-in-law, the sales pitch shifts smoothly into an explanation of how safe the car is to drive, its nerve-soothing cruise control, and general family-friendliness.

The salesperson isn't worried about whether you perceive the pitch as coherent. What matters is that somewhere there should be a topic that interests you. You will react to a stimulus that interests you and when it has been identified, everything else can be forgotten. The vendor uses every possible argument, one after the other and in bursts, unconcerned about any contradictions.[17]

8. Lots of salespersons and sales managers don't like to admit that sales can be completed by product information.

Although he is convinced he is indispensable, Mr. B. knows the importance of appealing, understandable, persuasive communication. Given his lack of familiarity with the Internet, it is unlikely that Mr. B. had a hand in designing the People of Freedom website, although he does constantly intervene in Mediaset television programs. But he certainly approved the party website.

Visitors to www.ilpopolodellaliberta.it on August 15, 2010, would have found a message in large type ("Take part in Operation Memory!") and could have accessed the "Album of the Can-Do Government."[18] They could have browsed, with or without background music, a list of the measures passed by the government from 2008 and 2010, arranged by subject: Income Support, Savings Security, Family-friendly Tax, Homes Plan, For the Working Woman, and so on. On the Democratic Party website, the same issues are buried in an avalanche of information, divided into thematic areas or bundled onto manifestos, press releases, and interviews. Anyone wanting to know what the Left would do in power, or hoping to find useful facts to win a cappuccino-fueled discussion with a Berlusconi-supporting barista, is visiting the wrong website. And the wrong café.

9. When a salesperson is involved, relationships are in fact more important than product knowledge, and salespersons who determine the client's needs in both product features and emotional needs will always win out.

Understanding clients. Mr. B. has been aiming—successfully—to do that for forty years, exploiting the same opportunities and the same mechanisms. He used to love the platform at company conventions. Today, he adores it. In 1968, when he was thirty-two, he sold apartments with the slogan: "When it's raining in Milan, the sun is shining in Brugherio!"[19] In 2006, he grabbed the microphone at the annual meeting of Confindustria, the employers' association, stood up, and repeated the self-same slogans: "Be positive! Be optimistic! An entrepreneur has a duty to be optimistic! Pessimism will get you nowhere! Don't believe the papers when they talk about decline. We haven't gotten poorer in the past few years!" And then on with a barrage of figures, jokes, and quotations.[20]

The client bought the package. An initially skeptical business community went over to Berlusconi.

10. Advertising, merchandising, and marketing are support functions for selling.

Mr. B. is a seducer. His desire to have his way with his interlocutors leads him to be flexible with the facts, to the point of touching up his autobiography. When he was at Publitalia, he claimed to have started his musical career in Lebanon (where he has never been), studied at the Sorbonne (where he has never studied), and won a national student rowing competition with CUS Milano (which never materialized). That's what's on the menu. One of the dinner guests at Palazzo Grazioli on May 25, 2010, was a Northern League stalwart from Busto Arsizio. "When I was a lad, I played on your town's team," Mr. B. told him. It's a pity that Pro Patria, the club concerned, has never had a member called Berlusconi.[21]

Giuseppe Berto once wrote, "It's easy to conclude that nations are gullible and fickle, since many of the individuals that comprise them are fickle and gullible. Now, gullibility is not a trait that princes worry about. Quite the reverse. Excessive fickleness, on the other hand, can irritate occasionally, but Machiavelli, who could not have been influenced by Stalin, says that all you have to do is arrange things so that 'when they don't believe any longer, you can force them to believe.'"[22]

A democratic, up-to-the-minute force, obviously. Undoubtedly, there is plenty of money, energy, and insistence in Mr. B.'s propaganda. Taking personal charge of an election campaign, pressing the flesh, and facing the cameras is not for everyone, particularly when you're past seventy. Brushing aside an accusation as having been "stirred up by the media" is one thing; doing it for sixteen years in a row is another thing altogether.

11. Sales can only be increased by certain things:

- Selling more of your existing products to your existing customers

- Adding new products
- Adding new customers

How can you keep your customers? You need to reassure them. This is one of the reasons Mr. B.'s visual imagery has remained unchanged, starting with the blue background. The color was left unclaimed under the First Republic, when the Christian Democrats were white, the Communists and Socialists red, the Republicans Green, and the neo-Fascist Italian Social Movement (MSI) red, white, and green like the Italian flag. Thanks to the attentions of image-maker Miti Simonetto, Silvio has created his own format: double-breasted suit (to hide the weight fluctuations); shades of blue (chromotherapy tells us it is the most relaxing color of all); lashings of makeup before public appearances; and an artificially dark, impeccably sculpted coiffure. You're more likely to hear a confession from Berlusconi than you are to see a hair out of place.

You need to prevent customers from being disappointed if you want them to buy more. This means pointing out the good things, glossing over the bad ones, and helping them to forget the broken promises.[23] To win new customers, you need to offer new features, so new features duly arrived. Years in government brought photographs with the great and the good of the planet, while unforeseen events like the Naples trash crisis and the earthquake at L'Aquila provided opportunities to show off spectacular new abilities.

12. Close the sale.

Elected in 1994, reelected triumphantly in 2001, edged out in 2006 after a surprisingly vigorous recovery, and elected for the third time in 2008 with a landslide majority.

If the competition doesn't get its act together, the salesman can rest assured he won't be heading into retirement for a good while yet.

CHAPTER SIX

The Zelig Factor

June 2010. Mr. B. touches down in Brazil and promptly poses in a green and gold soccer shirt. "Brazilian soccer isn't soccer, it's poetry." Italy's depressingly early exit from the South African World Cup is conveniently forgotten.

Our hero turns to Brazil's left-wing president, Luis Inácio Lula da Silva, and says, "We both come from the hard school of the workplace." The fact that one is a billionaire businessman and the other a worker is, of course, irrelevant.

Mr. B. adds, "The president told me he's been married for thirty-five years, but he has a roving eye." Doña Marisa Letícia da Silva, *primeira-dama do Brasil*, from Palazzago in the province of Bergamo, Italy, must be happy. Yet the remark was shrewd. In a sexually uninhibited nation, it showed he was in tune.

This remark highlighted the chameleon-like aspect of Silvio Berlusconi's character far more than the Sao Paulo satirists[1] who tried to press young women onto him, forgetting about his ever-present escort. Silvio adapts to his environment. Identifying with your interlocutors is a virtue in politics, but the ability actually to become them, like Leonard Zelig in the Woody Allen[2] film, is much rarer.

An anxiety to become everything in order to endure forever, in Italy and abroad. We jotted down a quick list in the introduction, but we could extend it. Macho with Vladimir Putin. Amusing with Merkel. Conservative with George W. Bush. Liberal with Barack Obama. European in Brussels and euroskeptic in London. A friend of Israel in Jerusalem, a friend of the Arabs in Cairo, and a friend of Iran in Tehran. An ordinary guy with Zapatero and a man of the world with Sarkozy, while pointing out that the French president owed Italy for giving him Carla Bruni. *"Moi je t'ai donné la tua donna"* was later diplomatically corrected to *"Tu sais que j'ai étudié à la Sorbonne"* (You know, I studied at the Sorbonne).

A family man with his five children (and two wives, while it lasted). A night owl with the night set. Youthful with the young. Wise with the old. A worker at the workplace. Entrepreneurial with the business community. Youthful with the young. *Rossonero* to the core with A.C. Milan supporters. Milanese with the people of Milan. Lombard with the people of Lombardy. Italian with people from southern Italy. And a Neapolitan among Neapolitans, with musical backing.

Anyone can learn to become a chameleon, but it takes talent to reach this level. Like Leonard Zelig taking on the identities of people around him, Mr. B. has that rare ability to mold himself to Italians' aspirations, depending on circumstance and contingent advantage. According to his first political biographer, Gigi Moncalvo, Mr. B.'s personal and professional history is a succession of magisterial imitations backed up by "exuberant hyperactivity," "boundless self-assurance," and an "absence of self-criticism of any kind."[3]

This is clear from various now-famous photos. From the 1950s: Mr. B. in a white cap on board a Costa Crociere cruise ship, pulling the mike stand toward him, like a real singer. From 1976: looking at a model of the Milano 3 development, like a real construction magnate. From 1978: at the presentation ceremony for Canale 5 television, like a real Brianza-born businessman. From 1980: doing an Alain Delon impression with hat, white suit, and cigarette, like a real actor. From 1987: holding an article by legendary sports journalist Gianni Brera, like the real chairman of a real soccer club. From 1994: posing on the Forza Italia platform, just like a real dancer.[4]

The most eloquent of the pre-politics pictures dates from the late 1970s and hangs in the office of Giuliano

Molossi, editor in chief of the *Gazzetta di Parma* newspaper. Silvio Berlusconi, who has just become a shareholder in *Il Giornale*, is walking down the Spanish Steps with editor in chief Indro Montanelli. Apparently, the younger man is unintimidated by the difference in age, height, bearing, and choice of dress. His spirits are as high as his shirt collar. Mr. B. is a young publisher, proud to have at his side a man he regards as a maestro.

When the two split up after Mr. B.'s entry into politics, Montanelli spoke about him with a mixture of repulsion, admiration, amazement, and fear. Montanelli said once after his new venture, *La Voce*, folded in the mid-1990s, "He has asked me for a meeting, but I'm not keen. I know what will happen: He'll turn up, burst into tears on the landing, throw his arms around me, and tell me he can't go on without me. And I'll believe him. And he'll have conned me."[5]

Montanelli understood that great salesmen and great seducers share this characteristic: They genuinely believe they are offering you the greatest product, or amorous experience. Some people fall for it, and generally they regret doing so.

Zelig becomes many things in the course of the film's seventy-nine minutes. Psychosomatic transformation multiplies his personality. He is a Republican among Republicans, a Democrat with the Democrats, aristocratic with the nobility, a doctor among doctors, a hoodlum with

gangsters, a black musician with blacks, a rabbi in the syna-
gogue, Chinese with the Chinese, a singer at the opera, and
a pitcher on the baseball diamond.

Zelig was driven by neurotic insecurity, Berlusconi by
an almost adolescent desire to be simultaneously part of the
group and the star of the show. Clothes, as any fifteen-year-
old will tell you, are crucial, and remain so throughout life.
We all dress for the occasion. Only a soldier, a Northern
League leader, or Peter Pan would wear green to a for-
mal reception. But Mr. B. is more scientific. His wardrobe
switches are never spontaneous.

The dark jacket/blue tie/pale shirt is his uniform for
official occasions, a reassuringly conformist signal. Double-
breasted jackets are his life insurance. The pullover thrown
over the shoulders, sleeves knotted at the front, smacks of
summer and is an Italian trademark. A jersey worn among
the flowers in his garden at Arcore says middle-class infor-
mality, while the black shirt worn under a dark jacket tells
Vladimir Putin it's time to get serious about the evening.

But there have been many other personalities in all
those years of politics. There's the Tony Manero–style white
suit and blue shirt, complemented by a gaggle of Cuban
dancers. There's the dress-optional party animal, with
scantily clad lovelies at his villa and the former Czech premier in the altogether. There's the dad running around the
grounds at Arcore with his son and dog ("Although he loves
animals of all kinds, Silvio Berlusconi rarely allows himself

to be photographed with them.")[6] There's the white-clad leader of the pack in Bermuda, with Gianni Letta, Fedele Confalonieri, Adriano Galliani, and Marcello Dell'Utri. Dell'Utri notes in his diary, "Strict diet, spiritual exercises, and profound reading matter. We were moved by pages from Francis Bacon and Plato."

Mr. B. has an awesome collection of headwear of all sizes, styles, and colors. In party-sponsored publications, Mr. B. can be seen wearing a blue Chinese-style beret among the cactuses at Villa Certosa; a military beret in Iraq; a range of hard hats (at the Blue Stream gas pipeline, in a factory, at a freeway construction site); a tambourine hat at a fashion show; a white cowboy hat in Texas; a rail guard's hat on a train; a yarmulke at a Jewish ceremony; a monumental fur hat in Russia; and the headline-grabbing bandana in which he welcomed the astonished Tony and Cherie Blair to Porto Rotondo.

Apart from the bandana, all of the above have been worn by the world's heads of state for many years. But if Deng Xiao Ping wears a Stetson on a visit to the United States, he's just a Chinese leader in a funny hat. If Angela Merkel puts on a hard hat to tour an automobile factory, she's a German lady complying with safety regulations. When Nicolas Sarkozy dons a rail guard's cap, he's a president mingling magnanimously with lesser mortals. Silvio is different. All it takes is a hat and a photographer, and he becomes a cowboy in Dallas, a worker in a factory, or a guard on the Freccia Rossa high-speed train. He probably thinks that he could drive it.

The term "transformism" has acquired hateful connotations in Italy. It was coined in 1882, when the leader of the liberal left, Agostino Depretis, formed an alliance with progressive right-wingers. One hundred thirty years on, transformism is an insult. "Transformist!" is tantamount to "traitor!" nowadays.

Attempting to adapt, however, is no big deal in an adaptable county. If you want to be me, you must like me, and faced with an audience of Italians, Mr. B. rarely gets it wrong. He flatters them, he wins their hearts, he loves them, and he leaves them. Silvio had this worked out when he was at Fininvest: "The main thing in the world of work is to be able to adapt to others. Other people don't have to adapt to us."[7]

The encounter with reconstruction workers at L'Aquila in the wake of the earthquake—an encounter that was filmed, criticized, and pilloried (not least in Sabrina Guzzanti's film *Draquila*)—illustrates his method. Mr. B. arrives, glances at the workers clinging to the scaffolding, and shouts up at them, "Where are the women? Are you all gay up there?" He goes on, "Well done, great job," and makes a few comments on the reconstruction. As he takes his leave, he reprises his initial theme, saying, "The next time I come, I'll bring you some girls from TV!"[8]

The workers don't protest. It's not that they're stunned into silence, reflecting that the prime minister really shouldn't be so flippant when visiting a town that has suffered. No, they're laughing and clapping. Celeb shock? Regard for an honored guest? Or a passion—for pretty women—shared by Italy's richest man and twenty hard hats living on thirteen hundred euros a month?

"How can you not be moved at a time like this . . .

[*applause—shouts from the audience: Go Silvio, go for it, you're one of us!*]

It's a solemn moment, an intense moment . . .

[*shouts from the audience: Turn on the light, Silvio!*]

Perhaps our nation really does need the light of hope and faith . . .

[*applause*]

On my way here, I thought about a crazy guy going to meet a bunch of other crazies . . .

[*applause—shouts from the audience: Silvio, Forza Italia! Otherwise we'll have to get out of Italy!*]

I don't think so, I don't think so . . . [*applause*] . . . I think we'll stay in this Italy, but we are determined to stay here as free men!

[*applause*]

Mulling over this craziness, which seems to have infected all of us, it struck me that what I once wrote in an introduction to a wonderful book—Erasmus of Rotterdam's *In Praise of Folly*—had again come true.

This is what I said: "The thesis expounded in these pages is correct. The most important, the wisest, the fairest decision, true wisdom, is not the one that derives from reason, or springs from the brain, but the one that comes from a farsighted, visionary folly."

[*applause*]

Rome, February 6, 1994

Mr. B. uses syntactically uncomplicated language. He talks straight. Unlike generations of Italian politicians before him, Mr. B. doesn't set much stock by Nietzsche's aphorism, "He who would like to appear profound to the multitude strives for obscurity." As Edmondo Berselli notes, since his first political rally Mr. B. has employed "a composite Italian, a pastiche of the ancient and the ultramodern mingling complexity and simplicity, sales technique and relentless flattery of his listeners."[9] The crucial thing "is that it work and that his audience find it appropriate."

Many years on, we can say that it works. Mr. B. tells people what they want to hear, in words they like listening to. Familiar words, which is why he has to change his linguistic code according to his audience.

THE BONOLIS CODE

Mr. B. adores words that have fallen out of fashion. They're his trademark. This is the technique made famous by television host Paolo Bonolis, who combines echoes of high school with sophisticated-sounding literary vocabulary. One of the Berlusconi nouns is *facinorosi* (ruffians), which delighted journalist Michele Serra ("It's a fabulous word. I hadn't heard it since Nino Nutrizio was editor in chief of *La Notte* [1952–1979]!"). Pet adjectives include *obsoleto* (obsolete), *liberticida* (freedom-denying), *consono* (commensurate), and *esteticamente plaudibile* (aesthetically praiseworthy). Classic linguistic Berlusconisms are *mi consenta* (allow me) and the use of the preterite tense, which is unnatural coming from a Lombard.

During a two-part television debate with Romano Prodi in 2006, Mr. B. came out with expressions like *tesi bislacca* (extravagant position), *frottola* (untruth), *spudoratezza* (impudence), and *adulterazione della realtà* (adulteration of the facts). He talked of his opponent's *danti causa* (predecessors in interest) and accused Francesco Rutelli of behaving *ignobilmente* (ignobly). At one point, he unsheathed the adjective *bieco* (boorish). Reflect on that. Who, in the grip of a hissy fit, would scream at someone: "You boor!"? The only possible response would be, "Foul knave! I challenge thee to a duel!"[10]

THE FOGAZZARO CODE

In 2007, Veronica Lario sent a record-straightening letter to *La Repubblica* newspaper. "I write to express my reaction to the statements made by my husband at the gala dinner for the Telegatti awards, where in addressing a number of the ladies present, he expressed sentiments that for me were unacceptable." In his reply, Mr. B. used the vocabulary of the nineteenth century, appropriate for a conservative electorate easily unsettled by charges of serial adultery: "I was *recalcitrante*" (kicking against the traces); "I am *giocoso* (playful), but also proud"; "even when a light-hearted comment emerges from my mouth, a *galante* (gallant) witticism, a moment's *bagattella* (whimsy)." It's straight out of the Antonio Fogazzaro novel *Piccolo mondo antico* (*The Little World of the Past*), although Fogazzaro didn't mention Telegatti.[11]

THE SOCCER STADIUM CODE

Mr. B. went into politics armed with the jargon of the soccer stadium: working-class, easy to understand, and redolent of recent success, since A.C. Milan was sweeping the board at the time: *discesa in campo, gioco di squadra, squadra di governo* (taking the field, team game, government team). To reach beyond Milan supporters, he chose the term *Azzurri* (Italian international players) for candidates and supporters of his Forza Italia (Go, Italy!) party. He didn't actually appoint himself the *presidente, allenatore, capitano* (chairman, coach, and captain), or *capocannoniere* (top scorer) of his new party, but he might as well have. Leonardo, the coach dropped by A.C. Milan in 2010 after a good championship, sums it up like this: "I left for reasons of incompatibility and style. Narcissus doesn't like anything he can't look at himself in. . . . I don't know why he talks about me so much."[12]

THE LOCKER ROOM CODE

During the 2001 election campaign, Mr. B. often told a story about a "gay man, a terminal AIDS victim" who was told to undergo sand therapy so he'd be "ready for the hereafter." The sense of humor (?) and language are out of a 1950s locker room, way beyond the bounds of good taste. But the locker room tone takes on softer shades when Mr. B. shifts to the vocabulary of José Mourinho's early days as manager of Inter Milan: "It's not easy cutting a deal with Bossi after what happened in 1994. I'd look like a complete dork."[13]

THE APPELIUS CODE

Mario Appelius was one of the most passionate—and least fact-bound—panegyricists of the (Italian) fatherland in the 1920s and 1930s. Whenever he feels like it, which is quite often, Mr. B. touches on this chord with results that can be grotesque or moving, depending on your inclination. Roberto Tartaglione has collected some of these verbal tics (in italics) for his school of Italian in Rome:

> "Italy *(we Italians are a genuine enigma for our foreign friends)* is portrayed with simple yet effective rhetoric: *peaceful, hardworking towns, marvelous Mediterranean intelligence, a construction site of work in progress,* and

an unsinkable nation where woman is the undisputed hub of family life, where young people are *our youngsters* or *Italy's young sons and daughters* who need to be assured of a future, where there are no poor, unemployed, or disabled, only *the less fortunate, the needy,* or simply those who *have been left behind.*"[14]

THE MARINETTI CODE

One of Mr. B.'s very favorite words—along with *protagonist, modern,* and *competition*—is *future* (building the future, certainty for the future, safeguarding the future, looking to the future with confidence, we are future-oriented, a future worthy of our past). For the only head of a European government born before the Second World War, the choice is an odd one. Make up your own minds whether Silvio is being farsighted or doing a bit of marketing.

The Zelig Factor has a corollary. Mr. B. doesn't just want to *be* everything; he is also convinced he can *do* anything. Yet again, he is reflecting an Italian stereotype. In Italy, admitting you can't do something is much more embarrassing than owning up to being dishonest.

Before embarking on a political career, Mr. B. tried his hand at industry, finance, publishing, retail distribution, construction, soccer, film, and television. He was resourceful and determined, where necessary using connections, ploys, and shortcuts in a very Italian fashion, albeit on an industrial scale. Yet his success cannot be explained away by connections, ploys, and shortcuts alone. Milano 2 is a fine example of urban development; Mediaset has succeeded where other, equally scruple-free, broadcasters have failed; and A.C. Milan has won many titles in Europe, where good connections count for very little.

The belief that he is omni-skilled has prompted Mr. B. to get involved with many other things in the course of his life, from office decor and his collaborators' dress code to the flower arrangements for international summits and the studio backdrops for television shows. (Long-serving journalist Enzo Biagi once said, "If he had boobs, he'd do the continuity announcements as well."[15]) This is another typically Italian trait. A desire to make ourselves useful, combined with an often unfounded conviction of competence, tempts us into rash adventures, where unselfishness is laced with ostentation.

If Haiti is struck by an earthquake, Mr. B. sends civil protection chief Guido Bertolaso, just as you or I would send our plumber to a friend grappling with a burst pipe. If Russia is ravaged by wildfire, Mr. B. sends fire planes to Medvedev, presenting the gesture as a personal favor. This restless energy has the effect of multiplying our hero's personalities. Compulsive intervention—the *ghe pensi mì* ("I'll sort it out" in Milanese dialect) Mr. B. trotted out on his return from one trip[16] was not a sound bite, but a confession—fuses with a desire to be liked by his interlocutors as he adopts their mannerisms and tastes. The resulting performances can be awesome.

At the Coldiretti farmers' convention in 2009, he was offered some mortadella so he could taste the quality of the product. Mr. B. grabbed the tray, hopped down from the platform, and started serving the audience himself.[17] And whose voice was it describing the beauties of Italy on the *Magic Italy* (sic) commercial in 2010? Mr. B.'s. Did he intend to take over the tourism portfolio as well as the mandate for economic development? No. He was simply convinced he was the Italian who is best-known and most admired abroad. It looked impossible to do any worse than Francesco Rutelli[18] in this respect, but Mr. B. had a go, proving that narcissism in Italy cuts across the party divide and is frequently inversely proportional to results.

Massimo Giannini once wrote, "There is no private vice, public virtue, cultural trend, or popular ethos that the man from Arcore has not simultaneously anticipated or expanded in his dizzyingly mysterious hall of mirrors, where it was, and still is, increasingly hard to distinguish who is reflecting what."[19]

Ernesto Galli della Loggia wondered, "Is the premier's behavior the reason for the lack of restraint, or rather the out-and-out vulgarity, that seems to typify current Italian public discourse? Or are those Berlusconian characteristics a manifestation, albeit an extreme one, of a more widespread transformation that involves the whole of our society?"[20]

The bottom line is this: If Zelig imitates a new Italian, and we find that new Italian puzzling, is it right to take issue with Zelig?

The answer is we can't forgive him, since our Zelig is a leader and, as such, has a duty to lead. On the other hand, Mr. B. often gives the impression he is chasing fashions, moods, and bad habits. There have been no amusing exhortations to pay our taxes, but there have been plenty of quips about lust and the other deadly sins.

He indulges our not always irreproachable instincts, and then reassures us by doing the same.

Some claim that Mr. B.'s abilities are even greater. They allege he encourages our baser instincts with commercial television, which quickly became the paradigm for state-owned channels. Nobody thinks he planned all this. No one believes that in the late 1970s, Mr. B. decided to mold the millions of new Italians who would vote for him fifteen years later.

Not least because if he had, he wouldn't be Zelig. He'd be Mephistopheles.

CHAPTER SEVEN

The Harem Factor

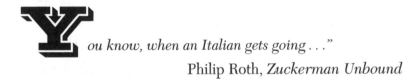

ou know, when an Italian gets going..."

Philip Roth, *Zuckerman Unbound*

Casoria, a suburb north of Naples. A Sunday evening in April.
Mr. B. arrives at a young woman's eighteenth birthday party.
"We've got a surprise for you!" squeals the birthday girl's
mother. The lights go off, and our hero strides into the room.

A true scene-stealer's entrance. Mr. B. is not content
with events where heads of government are lionized. He
knows that behind the applause lies habit, and beneath
the fine words is hypocrisy. But at Villa Santa Chiara, an
events complex on Naples' Circumvallazione beltway, the

amazement in everyone's eyes is unalloyed. If he could have materialized in the room without opening the door, as Someone Else did in the Bible, Mr. B. would have done so gladly.

"I call him Prime Minister, but occasionally what comes out is *papi* (daddy)," Noemi Letizia, the young woman concerned, would explain later. Mrs. Berlusconi focused firmly on that side of things ("I can't stay with a man who consorts with underage girls!"). Newscasts on public and private television, with one or two exceptions, were silent. Popular magazines played up the celeb value of the incident. Only the newspapers pointed out several curious contradictions.

It is not true that Mr. B. saw Noemi "only in the presence of her parents," as he claimed. She was photographed with him at a dinner at Villa Madama with movers and shakers from the fashion business, to whom she was introduced as "an intern, the daughter of dear friends from Naples." Later, Ms. Letizia was a guest at Villa Certosa in Sardinia, along with about thirty or so other young women. Nor is it true that her father, Benedetto Letizia, is "a long-standing Socialist and Bettino Craxi's driver." The former premier's son, Bobo Craxi, said, "My father's driver was named Nicola, he was from Veneto, and he's dead." According to Noemi's former boyfriend, the circumstances of their meeting were different: Noemi had a screen test with TG4 news director Emilio Fede for a job as a *meteorina*, or weather girl, and came to Mr. B.'s attention when he glanced at her photo book.[1]

Scandalous? Could be. Weird? You bet. The Mr. B. who turned up at a party on the outskirts of Naples, complete with bodyguards and a rearranged schedule, was not hoping to pass unobserved. The impact on those who witnessed this miracle—Italy's richest, most powerful man turning up at a birthday party in Casoria!—was just too tempting. *The Great Gatsby* is a better guide to this story than any essay by historian Gaetano Salvemini.

Moreover, many Italian males find the story reassuring. It fuels daydreams and provides justification for inexcusable yearnings. Perhaps not for running around with teens—not many kids want to be seen with seventy-year-olds—but at least for being tempted by hookers, watching the wrong television channels, or gazing at girls coming out of school. Mr. B. had few defenders after this episode, but there were plenty of embarrassed silences. That was good enough.

He might have pointed out how at exactly the same age, seventy-two, Johann Wolfgang Goethe became infatuated with seventeen-year-old Ulrike von Levetzow, to whom he dedicated *Elegy to Marienbad* ("Now I am far! And what would best befit the present minute? I could scarcely tell; . . . Yearnings unquenchable still drive me on . . ."). The young woman responded to Goethe's attentions, attracted to a man so successful his servant could make money by secretly selling his hair.[2] Today, it is not easy to invoke a parallel. Noemi is not Ulrike; Casoria is not Marienbad; Goethe wasn't writing for *Chi* magazine; and there isn't enough of Mr. B.'s hair for the servants to get rich.

✿

Decoding Berlusconi's obsession with women—it would be an understatement to say he "likes" them—is important. It enables us to see why the Harem Factor has not merely failed to tarnish his image, but actually continues to help him personally and politically.

His passion is boundless—rarely does he appear in public without making some erotic allusion or compliment—and seems to have several strands: the idealization of youth, the commercial value of beauty, the appreciation of women, and male pride. And what remains of lust, of course.

Let's start with youth, a weakness of the entire aging West, not just of one man born in Milan in the fall of 1936, year XIV of the Fascist era. Silvio is no Dorian Gray, although he uses television as a portrait. For advertising agencies, the youth obsession is a question of economics, but for Mr. B. it is a psychological crutch. He gets depressed with people his own age, except for a few friends, but a gaggle of young beauties[3] makes him as happy as the hero of a story by Boccaccio. It's another respect in which the ruler resembles the ruled. The fathers who make passes at their daughters' girlfriends, and the mothers who hope to be mistaken for them, are classic Italy.

There are many ways of trying to slow the passage of time. Some people meditate; others prefer nightclubbing. October 2008, the Lotus Club in Milan. Mr. B. strolled in at two in the morning and stayed for five hours. "If I get three hours' sleep, I still have the energy to make love for three more," he said at the door. "I have to go to work in an hour, but I feel fresh. I was at the all-night event in Paris, but then a friend invited me to this party and I couldn't turn him down."[4] Why does he do it? Ferruccio de Bortoli may have stumbled on the answer when he asked him, "Was it wise to go to Noemi's party at Casoria?" Mr. B. replied, "If I stopped going to these things, I wouldn't feel the same any more."[5]

The anxiety is socially acceptable, humanly understandable, and politically digestible. Many Italian men are held back by morals, decorum, their wives, or exhaustion, but not Mr. B. He sees himself as Gabriele D'Annunzio, the flamboyant man of letters, and is unencumbered by a sense of the ridiculous. "Don't worry, young lady, I'm single again," he said to a dancer at dinner in Sofia with Bulgarian prime minister Boyko Borisov, on an official visit to unveil an equestrian statue of Giuseppe Garibaldi. "Go and speak to the priest, the pharmacist, and the doctor," he told candidates for the 2008 general election. "I'm on excellent terms with pharmacists, and not because I buy Viagra from them. We don't need it."[6] That "we" is a nudge and a wink to the entire male electorate.

Silvio asks women for their phone numbers. When a woman is dressed to kill, he pays her a compliment (even if the woman is Michelle Obama), and he tells younger women they should go out with older men. When he wants to make a real looker smile, he whispers to her that she's a "woman to marry." That's what he told Mara Carfagna, infuriating his wife Veronica, as we have seen.[7] You could call it a case of a rooster being savaged by a brood hen after behaving like a peacock while handing out the Telegatti (Golden Cat) awards: More proof that Italy is a zoo. But the issue is even more intriguing, and more complicated.

Mr. B. reflects an eternal Italy of well-worn pick-up lines, endless erotic stimulation, and sincere compliments. Italians don't look at other people. They see them. And if those people are wearing short skirts and figure-hugging blouses, the inspection is that much more thorough, which can be irritating or gratifying, depending on the inspector and the occasion. Just ask Mr. B.'s supporters, or indeed some of his more sincere detractors. The man says into the microphone exactly what millions of Italian males say at the bar. It's not off-putting, because when the powerful are outrageous, it sounds like spontaneity.

Okay, some might say. All that might explain why Italian men go along with him, but why do women vote for him?

Well, these are waters Italian women know well. Mr. B.'s look is no different from the once-over they get from adolescents, advertising execs, and assorted men in the street. Nearly all women put up with this. Some even feel flattered. It never occurs to them that most, if not all, of those looks seal their status as second-class citizens. Women in Italy have more difficulty finding a job, get paid less, and struggle for promotion. But until they reach a certain age, they reckon they can win this game. In the long term, though, the house always wins. All you can do is delay the moment of defeat.

And there's another factor. Mr. B.—the sultan, the knight in white armor, the connoisseur, and the admirer— is genuinely curious about women. He often remarks on details of makeup, dress, and accessories. Or he expresses curiosity of a sexual nature, sometimes without sexual overtones. It happened back in his television days. When Lorella Cuccarini celebrated a quarter century on the small screen, she reminisced, "To think that Berlusconi criticized my bust. He said I was the only one of his stars who didn't have the measurements he likes." It was the most-read article on Corriere.it on July 24, 2010. Italy was fascinated by the head of government's opinion on a figure, albeit one belonging to a TV host, not the national economy.

Mr. B.'s attentions are not restricted to younger women, although he does have a preference for youth.

He promised a set of new teeth to Signora Anna, a seventy-three-year-old victim of the Abruzzo earthquake (the incident was duly recorded by TG1 news, which omitted to mention that the two were the same age).

He came off the platform unscathed, having called his middle-aged female supporters "the menopause brigade" (some even applauded).

He cooed at education minister Mariastella Gelmini ("How pretty you are! You look so young!").

He congratulated the chair of the Confindustria employers' association, Emma Marcegaglia, in his own ineffable way. ("Yesterday evening, she came to see me at the prime minister's office. A functionary told me, 'There's a hottie from TV to see you.'")

He became visibly excited at a Red Cross nurse marching past in the June 2 Festival of the Republic parade.[8]

Roberto Velatta wrote to me from Varallo Sesia, "I'm eighty now, but I worked as a steward on Costa cruise liners, and I was able to get to know Berlusconi pretty well during my shifts in the ballroom. Apart from being a good singer, he was a very congenial communicator, especially with the women. I'm happy to read about his success in business and politics, so if you can, try and treat him a little better."[9] I replied okay, on one condition. Next time you're in Milan, come and tell me about the young Silvio on those cruise ships. Was he already promising women he'd make them government ministers one day?

✣

Then, of course, there's masculine pride, an ancient, pre-political emotion that lives on in Italy, and in Europe, often artfully disguised. Woman as companion, entertainer, walking admirer, rapt audience, and sleek trophy.

For instance, what happened to twenty-eight-year-old Federica Gagliardi after the G20 summit, where she managed to get her photo taken with Obama and Sarkozy? Let's find out: "The Italian delegation replied that the woman met the prime minister during the campaign for the Lazio regional elections and expressed a desire to take part in an international mission. Her request was able to be granted because one of the premier's secretaries was unavailable."[10] The reply was mind-boggling, but the public just chuckled and accepted it.

Courtship, a ritual that in other cultures is viewed with suspicion, survives in Italy. "When you pay someone a compliment, it must be true. Politics is like chatting up women," explained Mr. B. to Confindustria's youth section, before suggesting a quote from Tagore as a seduction technique: "Dreams flit from your dark eyes like swallows from their nest in spring." He added, "Use with caution."[11]

His actual, or apparent, female conquests are campaign medals and marketing tools. His Turkish girlfriend comes in handy in Istanbul, and French women are a guarantee of success in Paris. ("I'm really popular with the French. Look at how many French girlfriends I've had!")[12] All delivered tongue in cheek, to leave himself an exit strategy. Yet overall, the impression is that these crowd-teasing lines are sincere. Deep in their hearts, Italians struggle with the same dilemma.

For as long as he could, Mr. B. strove to keep the public image of his marriage traditional. There was no shortage of family photographs. But he did have a theory on the sincerity of hypocrisy: "I'll give you a naughty answer. I have often been faithful," he said in the course of a radio interview in 2006, when he also announced he had taken a vow of chastity[13] in support of an election victory he missed by 25,000 votes out of 38 million.[14] A temporary vow, obviously, just as some people diet between meals and still expect to slim.

Now and again, Mr. B. slips up and says something nerve-janglingly awful, or repeats himself, but you get the feeling that it's more from a lack of imagination than out of tactlessness. Among the ruins of earthquake-devastated L'Aquila in May 2009, Mr. B. asked Lia Beltrami, the Trento provincial councilor with responsibility for solidarity, "Can I fondle madam a bit?" On a visit to Novedrate in the province of Como, home of the e-Campus online university created by Francesco Polidori, founder of the CEPU private exam prep chain, he is reported to have said, "They're always accusing me of surrounding myself with brainless lookers. But here are some great-looking girls who graduated with full marks yet look nothing like Rosy Bindi."[15] Ms. Bindi, who is deputy leader of the Chamber of Deputies, grumbled, "It's a sign that the empire is crumbling."

Wrong. The empire is striking back, and again where we are weakest.

Vanity fuels Mr. B.'s engine, and audiences are his gas stations of choice. A worldview emerges through the applause, the banter, and the anecdotes. Mr. B. is not just drawn to beauty: He sees it as key to success, to building a career, and to social advancement.

He had some memorable—because it was sincere—advice for a brunette who asked him how a young couple with no stable job "could afford to pay off a home loan, or start a family." The answer was "Well, first of all the young couple—and this is the advice that I give you as a father—should seek out the son of Berlusconi, or someone else who doesn't have that kind of problem. With a smile like yours, you could do it." Political blasphemy, anywhere. But many Italians don't just share this view. If they have a pretty daughter, they tell her, "Find yourself a rich man while you can."

Mr. B. knows full well that young, attractive female ministers will get more attention than their middle-aged male colleagues. Artful leg-crossing earns more media coverage than elegant oratory. Obviously, politicians everywhere know this, from Carla Bruni Sarkozy's Elysée to the American Midwest, where Sarah Palin won more votes for her embonpoint than for her brains. The difference is that Mr. B. says so in public, without blushing. At one party conference, he began a speech, "I can see some delegates of remarkable aesthetic achievement in the front row. As is common knowledge, I am in love with my wife, but I haven't lost my aesthetic sense and there are some fantastic legs down there."[16] With hindsight, we can say that the second part of the statement was more sincere than the first.

This commercial consideration of beauty extends to men. Presenting his A.C. Milan soccer squad in summer 2010, Mr. B. first pointed out that "with me on the bench, you would have won the championship" and then claimed that new purchase Mario Yepes "is a tough defender and good-looking, too, which always helps," while striker Marco Borriello "is such a looker that women fans are going to fall in love with him." What about the new manager, Massimiliano Allegri? "We couldn't have given Dolce and Gabbana a better body to hang our kit on. He's a very good-looking guy, and he'd be perfect as a film star, but he's a fine coach."[17] Thank goodness for that.

Finally, there is lechery.

When he was speaking to a group of Italian and Brazilian business people in Sao Paulo in June 2010, our hero claimed to be suffering from memory loss. He said, "In the hotel this morning, I fancied a quickie with the chambermaid. She objected, 'But Prime Minister, we did it only an hour ago.'" A year later, he admitted into another microphone (the Berlusconi equivalent of a confessional), "I'm no saint; you've all figured that out."[18]

Yes, Prime Minister. We don't know how, we've no idea when, and we're not sure to what extent, but perhaps we've figured out why.

CHAPTER EIGHT

The Medici Factor

It would be interesting to ask those women why they accepted fifty euros to take part in a Muslim recruitment show in Rome for Muammar Qaddafi.[1] Babysitters earn more. As religious bit players, they didn't get much, put up with plenty, and embarrassed their country. For what it matters. If it still matters.

Mr. B. was true to form. For decades, he has been saying that the customer is always right. The rule holds true for everyone: crotchety advertisers, fickle voters, awkward allies, and irksome guests. One such guest was Qaddafi, who has an uncomplicated take on modernity. He preens, others admire; he talks, others listen; he gives orders, others obey.

Catholics were shaken by the Colonel's provocation ("Europe should embrace Islam") and for once appeared united in their reaction. The Catholic daily *Avvenire* was evangelically irritated. ("A regrettable farce.") Even Comunione e Liberazione, an organization ever obsequious to power, objected. Maurizio Lupi and Mario Mauro, respectively the People of Freedom's deputy group leader in the Chamber of Deputies and group leader in the European Parliament, wondered, "Is it still a good idea to offer Italy as a stage for the Libyan leader's shows?"

In contrast, the public's reaction was predictable. Amazement, not indignation. Curiosity, not questions. Irony, not protest. Italians observed the silent battle of the hair dye being waged behind the pledges of friendship, took note of the commercial agreements, admired the Berber horsemen, and listened to the Libyan leader's proclamations. Then Italy had other things to do.

Why was the Qaddafi show tolerated?[2] Officially, the reason is that only Italy is so close to Libya and has so many interests there! The unofficial reason is that we don't mess with those in power. Whether power is called Signore, Prince, King, Emperor, Duke, Duce, President, or Colonel, we have been putting up with it for centuries. We might satirize, circumvent, or hoodwink power, but we don't mess with it.

In Italy, the powerful do not have to exercise their power with restraint, as they do in other Western democracies.

They can flaunt it. Many will regard the potentate's excesses as a source of amusement, or even pride. A Russian czar or an Arab sheik has similar privileges. President Medvedev can turn up at Cervinia and wash down his lunch with champagne at one thousand euros a bottle; Qaddafi can turn Rome into his personal television studio; and Mr. B. has no need to cover up what he has or what he does, parties and pretty girls included. That's why the prime minister's office in Palazzo Chigi has got on so well with Tripoli and the Kremlin since the current tenants took up residence.

Libero newspaper ran a series of supplements entitled "Berlusconi tale e quale" ("The Real Berlusconi"), and subtitled "Vita, conquiste e passioni di un uomo politico unico al mondo" ("Life, Conquests, and Passions of a Unique Politician"). Number five has the most illuminating cover. The issue is dedicated to Berlusconi the construction magnate and creator of the Milano 2 development. Silvio is hunkering down among the crocuses at his villa in Arcore. He's sniffing one of the flowers and casting a critical eye over the others. Page 95 reveals why: "I select the flowers for my gardens," reads the caption.

> Out of the automobile steps the man, Berlusconi, who personally looks after every detail, including the planting of many dozens of tall trees. Under his direction, the trees were skillfully situated, but it is often asked how many of them will survive the shock of being

transplanted. . . . In fact, this is not a problem because one of Silvio's many innovations has been to stipulate an agreement between Milano 2 and a series of nurseries up and down Italy to ensure that any trees that fail to take root will be replaced. Not many people know that Berlusconi has a first-class knowledge of botany, born of a passion he has always had for plants, flowers, and nature in general.

Issue number fourteen—in a series published by a theoretically independent newspaper—features a photograph of "Silvio, the minister, and the little boy." Mr. B. is stretching a Sistine Chapel–style finger toward a clearly astonished one-year-old. The caption tells us:

> An emblematic image of Silvio Berlusconi's attitude to the new generations. Both he and Stefania Prestigiacomo, minister for the environment and territory, hold out a hand to the little boy in the arms of his father, who has explained the problems he faces to the representatives of government.

It is pointless to deny that the images and language are reminiscent of dictatorship-style hagiography. In 1980s Romania, Nicolae Ceausescu was portrayed in very much the same manner. The parallel with the Conducator was suggested even by Silvio's long-standing friend, Fedele

Confalonieri. In one interview he called Berlusconi ". . . an enlightened despot . . . a *good* Ceausescu, but decidedly anomalous as a democratic politician."[3] Another analogy comes from longer ago, but closer to home. There's not much difference from the communications point of view between "Italy's first farmer," the bare-chested Mussolini among the wheat, and "Italy's first gardener," the sweatered Berlusconi among the flowers. Both are posing, pretending to be what they are not.

Yet both these parallels, while tempting, are misleading. You don't have to study communism or fascism to understand many Italians' take on Berlusconi. You need to go further back, to the days of the *signorie*, the autocratic medieval lordships.

The signorie came after the *comuni* (municipalities), appearing in thirteenth-century northern Italy and disappearing almost entirely by the end of the fourteenth century. A signoria involved rule by an individual instead of a group, endlessly at war with other groups, classes, factions, guilds, or families. Many Italians greeted the new development favorably, then as now.

The signoria shared a key characteristic with the *comune*: the consensus of the people. Mr. B. has certainly never lacked consensus, which has been the basis for all his claims, including authority to fire the leader of one of the branches of Parliament, or contest the legitimacy of magistrates to judge him.

In the days of the signoria, consensus was expressed by acclamation. Today, we have elections. Giuseppe Prezzolini wrote in his *The Legacy of Italy*, first published in the United States in 1948, then in France in 1951, in Spain in 1956, and only in 1958 in Italy:

> The common people, who had played little or no part in the communal government, derived some advantages from the *signorial* government, and constituted its most faithful supporters against the discontent, disorder and conspiracies of the dispossessed upper classes. . . . The *signorie* represent a liberation from the oppressive power of a middle class of bankers, merchants, artisans, industrialists, and from the perpetual conflict among these classes. However strange it may seem, the *signore* is always supported by the lower classes and opposed by the upper classes. The people prefer to have dealings with a permanent ruler than with an unstable minority.[4]

It is going too far to maintain that the upper classes have been expropriated by Berlusconi, and it is extravagant to claim that today they are capable of plotting. Yet wolf-crying about the *poteri forti*[5] ("strong powers") smacks of a very old tactic: setting yourself up as a champion of the lower—by income, education, or social status—classes, and fomenting resentment against the upper classes. The former are more numerous, so the tactic works, whether in a medieval piazza or a modern democracy.

Prezzolini goes on:

The most typical example is the formation of the
signoria of the Medici which lasted for centuries. From
Salvestro to Cosimo, the Medici family always espoused
the cause of the little man against the members of its
own merchant class. This concern for their interests is
felt by the populace and is rewarded by loyalty and a
desire for continuation of the same ruling power.

The concern of the medieval signore was not disinter-
ested: The mask of republican claims concealed personal
advantage. The populace knew this, and found justifications. Only one thing was, and is, never forgiven in rulers:
squabbling, which remained the prerogative of the ruled.

[The signore] stands alone and dominates the scene in
the same way an imposing statue does a city square. He
is isolated by his strength, intelligence, and ambition
and especially by his suspicions. . . . His minister may be
a spy, his chancellor a traitor, his captain in the pay of
the enemy. What he fears from others, he has done or is
preparing to do, to others.

Again, the parallel is surprising. In his many years of
political activity, Mr. B. has shown hc is capable of loyalty,
amnesia, forgiveness, spite, exaltation, and rejection. He

has done nothing to pave the way for an orderly passage of power. The party is a mere pedestal for the signore. Its task is to support his monument.

In 2008, Italians were puzzled, but not astonished, by the appointments of Mariastella Gelmini as minister of education, universities, and research, and of Mara Carfagna as equal opportunities minister. Ms. Gelmini, born in 1973, has a high-school diploma she acquired at a private church-run school, a degree in law from Brescia, plus a change of residence to more relaxed Reggio Calabria in order to pass her bar exam, and some experience in local politics. Ms. Carfagna, born in 1975, studied dance and piano. She has a law degree from Salerno, came in sixth in the Miss Italia beauty contest, appeared occasionally on television, and published one of those calendars[6] you don't consult to check what day it is. Judgments on their respective performances as ministers do not make their appointments any more explicable. We can only accept them for what they are: the choices of the signore, who picks and promotes, but does not explain.

In Italy, the powerful have no need to justify their actions. The current electoral law—defined by its inventor, Roberto Calderoli, as "a dirty trick"[7]—decrees protected lists and complete freedom to add or remove candidates. The beneficiaries are Mr. B. and the heads of the other parties. This is one of the reasons why the Italian Parliament shelters twenty or so convicted criminals, as well as about

eighty individuals under investigation, on trial, or exon-
erated by a statute of limitations. The *Parlamento Pulito*
(Clean Parliament) bill promoted by Beppe Grillo and
signed by 350,000 citizens, gathers dust in the Senate.[8]

Discretion has morphed into absolute power in the
People of Freedom: Those Mr. B. likes are in; anyone he
dislikes is out, or marginalized. Submission is the rule. It
doesn't necessarily mean that beneficiaries are undeserving,
but there is no way of checking whether they are, or inter-
vening if they aren't.

Criteria for selection are impenetrable. A.C. Milan
soccer club's physiotherapist, Giorgio Puricelli, and Mr. B.'s
personal dental hygienist, Nicole Minetti, were elected to
the Lombardy regional council in 2010; the Arcore surveyor,
Francesco Magnano, is Lombardy's regional council cabi-
net member for territorial attractiveness and promotion;
Barbara Matera, a Miss Italia finalist, RAI television continuity girl, showgirl on the *Mai dire gol* and *Chiambretti
c'è* TV programs, actress in the *Carabinieri 7* TV serial
and "VIP skater" in the *Notti sul ghiaccio* talent show, has
been a member of the European Parliament since 2009.
Now they're saying that master necktie maker Maurizio
Marinella could be a candidate for mayor of Naples.

Past beneficiaries include Massimo Maria Berruti, for-
merly of the financial police, who carried out an inspection
of Berlusconi's Edilnord company in 1979, left the service,
and joined Fininvest before his election to the Chamber of
Deputies in 1996. Romano Comincioli, a school friend and

founding member of Fininvest and Forza Italia, has been a senator since 2001. Salvatore Sciascia, former director of tax services at Fininvest, deputy chairman of Mr. B.'s Idra real estate company, and chair of the family's Quattordicesima holding company, has been a senator since 2008. Alfredo Messina, deputy chairman of Mediolanum and chair of the Mediolanum Assicurazioni insurance company, has been a senator since 2008. Paolo Berlusconi's ex-wife, Martella Bocciardo, has been a member of the Chamber of Deputies since 2006.

Trusted lawyers Niccolò Ghedini, Gaetano Pecorella, Piero Longo, and Massimo Baldini are all in Parliament, the first two in the Chamber of Deputies and the others in the Senate. Carlo Taormina, one of Mr. B.'s top lawyers until 2008, was a deputy with Forza Italia from 2001 to 2006, the junior minister of the interior who drafted the Cirami law on legitimate suspicion, and is no longer in Parliament after what he calls "a moral crisis." ("I know only too well how Berlusconi asks his lawyers to make laws tailored to his needs because up till a few years ago, he was asking me.") Personal physicians Antonio Tomassini and Umberto Scapagnini feature. The former has been a senator since 1996, and today chairs the Senate health commission, while the latter, elected mayor of Catania in 2000, hit the headlines for calling Berlusconi "technically almost immortal."[9]

Some are able; others less so. Some have sought to live up to their leader's largesse, while others deny he was the reason for their success. Gabriele Albertini—a former mayor of Milan chosen by Mr. B.—today talks about "a ruling class that comes not from the grass roots, but from a wave of the Prince's magic wand," pointing the finger at "a court of unelected nominees that defends tooth and nail the power bestowed by the Prince, but not legitimized by the people."[10]

Albertini can say so, from his exile in the European Parliament. Once, a remark like that would have condemned him to a dungeon on some remote Mediterranean island.

Italian history is studded with suspect eulogies. No one gets accused of toadyism. There's always someone else with an even more superlative superlative. One July evening in 2010, Mr. B. received the Grande Milano award.[11] The motivation cited the "astonishing farsightedness and ability," the "admirable example," and "exceptional human and entrepreneurial qualities" of a "statesman of rare ability" who was leading the nation toward "a supportive society based on love." The fact that the awardee and the awarder, chair of the provincial authority Guido Podestà, belonged to the same party, the former had selected the latter for his job, and the two had known each other since they were both working at Edilnord in 1976, provokes indignation in opponents yet is irrelevant to supporters. The most reasonable reaction—embarrassment—is absent. You either love the signore or oppose him.

A few weeks later that same summer, People of Freedom cofounder Gianfranco Fini had just been dismissed from the party. Mr. B. invited the party's women parliamentarians to the castle of Tor Crescenza, one of his summer residences in Lazio. "What superb earrings! As they say, the bigger the earrings, the bigger the desire!" Mr. B. joked to Nunzia Di Girolamo, the young party coordinator from inner Campania, serving her first session in Parliament. She had already been remarked on for entering Palazzo Grazioli with a mosaic by Campanian artisans portraying the prime minister with his mother, Rosa.[12]

When former minister Claudio Scajola was still in favor, he called Berlusconi "our Sun King."[13] He got the period, the title, and the country wrong. But he knew what he was talking about.

This is what we have called the Medici Factor. As we have seen, Florence's signoria is an excellent roadmap to the highways and byways of power in Italy. But there are good examples elsewhere. We don't know what Cosimo de' Medici, the first signore of Florence, actually looked like. No authentic representations have come down to us.[14] However, thirty-three portraits survive of Federico da Montefeltro, most of them commissioned by the man himself,[15] making him the most frequently portrayed man in Italy. Federico, duke of Urbino, was a master of product placement. A keen bibliophile, he inserted his likeness onto the pages of manuscripts so that the great classics would conserve his portrait for posterity.

Our modern signore is equally obsessive about his image. Whereas Federico posed for oil portraits, Silvio can choose between photographs and television. Both men share an awareness—their image has to be impressed on their contemporaries' collective imagination like a trademark—and an imperative: to show the product in its best light.

In fifteenth-century Montefeltro, court painters chose a profile to conceal the fact that the duke had lost an eye during a tournament in honor of Francesco Sforza in 1451. The upshot was that their attention concentrated on the duke's aquiline nose with its curious step-like protuberance, turning it into Italy's best-known facial appendage. Cologno Monzese and the other offices entrusted with looking after the image of *Il Dottore*, as Berlusconi is called by his collaborators and employees, do not have a Piero della Francesca on the payroll. Their aim is to make amends for "a physique that falls short of aspirations." Lack of height, baldness, and a build that journalist Giampaolo Pansa called *inquartato* (thickset) do not help.[16] But the public does not perceive the reality, only its representation.

One celebrated piece of touching up was a photograph taken on May 5, 2003, at the first section of the court of Milan, where Mr. B. was giving a spontaneous statement at the SME trial, in which he was under investigation for bribery. Cramped spaces meant photographers had to work from the back of the court. The shot, published by *Newsweek* on May 12, reveals our hero's extensive bald patch. On the cover of the May 15 edition of *Panorama*, published by the Berlusconi family's Mondadori company, the baldness has disappeared, to be replaced by a thick rug of dark hair.[17]

Mr. B. sets much store by this sort of thing. His obsession with appearances makes him human in a country that loves to admire itself in store windows while consoling those who approve of, or at least vote for, him. No admirer can tolerate an unworthy object of admiration. It would cast doubts on the admirer's judgment.

Silvio knows this and tries to live up to expectations. He doesn't have a military background, like Federico. Mr. B. comes from advertising and TV, where everything has to look perfect. You can see the sparse trees of Montefeltro behind Federico in his tempera on wood portrait, while behind Silvio there are party-blue backdrops, shelves of books, or cheering supporters. Both men are invariably depicted without a single gray hair, but the Signore of Arcore would never have permitted his best-known portrait to feature the four celebrated warts we see on the left cheek of the duke of Urbino, the legacy of a skin disease he suffered in his youth. Piero della Francesca wanted to be as realistic as the great fifteenth-century Flemish masters. The portrait painters at the court of Berlusconi tend more toward oleographs, like twentieth-century American illustrators.

I nearly forgot. The man who deprived Federico of one eye and condemned him to pose eternally in profile was called Guidangelo de' Ranieri. Before the fateful ride, he received a gold chain from the duke.[18] The woman who damaged Silvio's reputation, forcing him to admit in public habits he would rather have kept private, is called Patrizia D'Addario. She, too, may have received a pendant after the fateful ride.

Mr. B. has kept referring to the "party of love,"[19] receiving generous helpings of incredulity and suspicion in response. As is often the case, his insistence is driven by insight and tactics. The signore truly wants to be loved, and feels pain when he is not. He has no intention of changing his lifestyle, buddies, or decisions in order to win that love. He wants it. Period.

Alexander Stille, today a ferocious critic, describes the conclusion of his first meeting with Silvio Berlusconi in 1996:

> "You don't understand," he said as our talk came to an end, leaning back wearily on the white couch in his living room, as if gathering his strength for one final attempt to make me see the light. "I have achieved everything in life a man can hope for. I have nothing left to gain personally." He suddenly coiled his body forward, turning up his level of intensity several notches, as if to make a final pitch to a recalcitrant client: "I have had this amazing, unique experience and I want to make

a contribution to the nation. I can create, I can command, I can make myself loved."[20]

This conviction is both revealing of the man and an explanation for his success. Mr. B.'s desire for approval prompts him to seek consensus obsessively. For many voters, it is gratifying to know they can give the signore what he wants. Many of Mr. B.'s voters turn nasty when they think someone doesn't love him. For them, inconsistency is not an issue. What does disturb them—mightily—is the belief that the leader's good intentions might not be appreciated as much as they should be.

This frantic need for approval is almost certainly linked to his past activities. The inventor of the Milano 2 development wanted its residents to be happy. The owner of Standa supermarkets wanted satisfied shoppers. The chairman of A.C. Milan craved fans' affection. And the importer of *Dallas* and *Baywatch* dreamt of faithful viewers. Berlusconi the publisher would have liked soothing support from his papers when he went into politics. When it turned out not to be unanimous, he felt betrayed. Mr. B. strode into the *Il Giornale* newsroom on January 18, 1994. He didn't speak as a publisher to his journalists. Instead, this was a signore addressing his troops: "The day of the rapier is no more. It's time to unsheathe the saber."

Some of those present refused to join up, but you can always find mercenaries in Italy.

＊

This is why attention from abroad makes us uncomfortable. It looks like disrespect for the signore. Every Italian is familiar with this irritation, this embarrassment that shades into displacement. Not all of us want to admit to it.

In March 2010, BBC2 broadcast *The Berlusconi Show* on U.K. prime time television from 7:00 p.m. to 8:00 p.m. The man in the spotlight was depicted as a skillful businessman, a charismatic populist, an incorrigible womanizer, and a politician with dubious connections.

The aim was to portray the person, without tendentious exaggeration, but in doing so it presented insights that the British TV audience, for reasons of culture and tradition, found mind-boggling. If the British prime minister were discovered in Downing Street with a woman who was not his wife, and who was later revealed to be a prostitute, while he was awaited at the American embassy to celebrate the election of the new president of the United States, he would be forced to resign within the hour. In Italy, this simply does not happen.

If people abroad are aghast, and attack him, the signore can raise a shield—the Italian nation. "Discredit is thrown not just on the prime minister; it also sullies our products, our businesses, everything made in Italy," he roared to the business community in Monza in October 2009. "These absurd, ridiculous charges . . . cast aspersions on the prime minister, the nation, and our democracy!" he thundered to voters in Benevento.[21] It's a shame that eleven months later in Yaroslavl, Russia, Mr. B. accused Italian judges ("Oppression, something that is unacceptable in democracy"), heaped scorn on the leader of the Chamber of Deputies ("He wants his own little business"), and criticized the Italian constitution, before winding up with: "Putin and Medvedev are God's blessing on the Russian people."[22]

The identification of the signore with the nation is a temptation to be shunned. But Mr. B. will not listen to reason. Italian ambassadors are pressured into writing protests to foreign newspapers and ministers propose planet-wide strategies, such as Michela Vittoria Brambilla's "anti-detractor task force." In a democracy, power is strictly monitored and harshly criticized by the opposition, the electorate, and the media at home and abroad. Bill Clinton, George W. Bush, Tony Blair, Helmut Kohl, José Luis Rodríguez, and Jacques Chirac have all sustained violent personal attacks. Barack Obama got annoyed with Fox News, which had him in its crosshairs. Yet no one accused the critics, at home or abroad, of slandering the nation.

A Medici or a Montefeltro might have, though.

CHAPTER NINE

The T.I.N.A. Factor

In reality, you invented Berlusconi. He is the child of the demonization that has dogged him since he took the political field. He is the child of your unremitting denigration, your scorn for all he does, all he says, all he wears, all he thinks. He is the child of your intolerance for the only Boss whom you have attacked in recent decades, perhaps with the approval of other bosses. He is the child of the bad government of your governments, the vacuity of your leaders, and the cultural arrogance of your intellectual, judicial, and media castes. He is the child of everything you ascribe to him.[1]

Marcello Veneziani's polemic chooses to gloss over the failings of the Italian Right, but it does accurately capture some of the vices of the Left. It also helps us to see that the winners manage to win because the losers are determined to lose. Voting is a question of options.

"The Left loses not just because it is arrogant, presumptuous, and insincere," wrote Luca Ricolfi in *Perché siamo antipatici?* [*Why Are We Hard to Like?*]. "It also loses because it fails to understand Italian society, it cannot look at the world except through ideological glasses, it doesn't know how to get on with ordinary people, and it has completely lost the ability to listen and the desire to understand."[2]

Puglia's regional president Nichi Vendola, a man of the Left, appears to agree: "Berlusconi's strength lies in our weakness."[3]

Let's take a look at why this is: the Left's often insouciantly dismissed communist past; its divisions, self-importance, inadequacies, and guaranteed jobs for life; ambivalences, uncertainties, and a lack of clear programming; an inclination to exhort, where its adversary absolves; and an inability to perceive Italians' gut feelings, the ones Mr. B.'s ear has attentively monitored for years, skillfully interpreting their every modulation.

For forty-four years, from 1948 to 1992, the majority of Italians voted for Christian Democracy, or even the Socialist

Party, to keep the Communists out of power. When the Clean Hands investigations (1992-1993) buried both the Christian Democrats and the Socialists, the post-Communists—who emerged relatively unscathed for reasons about which every Italian has an opinion—could have chosen European social democracy, or taken the path mapped out by American Democrat Bill Clinton, who had recently arrived in the White House.

Things didn't go like that. Since then, the Left has indulged in a helter-skelter of ups, downs, diversions, shortcuts, names, and experiments of which voters have understood little, and enjoyed less. It has preached solidarity to a nation devoted to initiative, offered social redemption to people dreaming of entertainment, talked duty to rights-obsessed listeners, invoked a "new approach to planning" (without saying what the plans were) to a country that performs best in emergencies, and attempted to sell equality and fraternity to a nation that, if forced to borrow a noun from the French, opts for *liberté*, preferably in the sense of freedom to do whatever you want.

The impression is that the Left, unlike its opponent, really doesn't understand how much Italians have changed. The process of hedonizing Italy embraced the entire political spectrum. Young unmarried Communists would come home in the evening and glance at the scantily clad women on the *Drive In* show, just like their Christian Democrat counterparts. Mr. B. saw this at once and threw himself body and soul—in that order—into singing the praises of what was there. His opponents chose instead to shut both eyes and promptly fell asleep.

Romano Prodi and the Olive Tree Alliance's wake-up call worked because it was cautious: We will modernize, liberalize, and Europeanize Italy, but we won't make too much fuss. With Mr. Prodi torpedoed—twice, in 1998 and 2008— the Left set off on another round of noisy experiments, accompanied by the descant warblings of old-time hard-liner Fausto Bertinotti. He had clear ideas—it's a shame they were the wrong ones—and belonged to Communist Refoundation. The adjective enthuses one Italian in twenty and horrifies the other nineteen, which is why Mr. B. calls all his opponents "communists." Even though the label comes off straight away, some of the glue sticks.

Moreover, the Left in Italy has the bad habit of saying things it doesn't do, and doing what it doesn't say. Some Italians knew, many guessed, and others suspected that Mr. B. wanted to see the end of Michele Santoro's hostile TV show *Annozero*. What left everyone stunned was the way the victim cashed in on his own surrender. The press reported that Santoro's payoff from RAI television was worth several million euros. His rival host, Bruno Vespa, commented sarcastically, "Being persecuted is very profitable."[4] In the end, the show wasn't suspended, and the deal came to nothing, but many floating voters decided the Left wasn't telling it straight, whereas the Right at least preaches what it practices. Even when what it preaches is nothing to be proud of, and that, it has to be said, is often the case.

In his book *La Cricca* [*The Clique*], Sergio Rizzo quotes part of an interview by Luca Telese with Clelio Stracquadanio, a People of Freedom deputy and founder of the online newspaper *Il Predellino*. Question: "Why do your leaders deny that the justice laws are personalized?" Answer: "They're wrong to deny it. It should be stated clearly that we are in favor of personalized laws."[5] And after eight chapters, we know who the person concerned is.

You could say many things to someone with that opinion, not all of them polite. But can you deny that he is sincere? Such frankness pays in Italy's primitive political stock market. There is a frankness dividend, and a hypocrisy coupon. The incorrigible Left goes for the coupon, and then wonders why its capital dwindles and investors flee.

> The political agenda of the new Democratic Party is desolately empty, a long way from what Marx demanded or the spirit of progressive Catholics. In short, they do not have a single, comprehensible word to say on work, benefit payments, public debts, or euthanasia. . . . I'm sorry to say so but, especially at the present time, a Left like this is of no use to the country.
>
> *Guido Bocchetta*

If the initial trend in the last election is confirmed (workers who used to vote for the Left now vote for the

Northern League), it will ram home yet again a concept so simple as to be almost silly. People who spend their lives trying every day to make ends meet at the end of the month couldn't care less whether Berlusca has one or two women on the side. It's the yacht-owning comrades preaching about true values worth fighting for who really irritate them.

Domenica Grangiotti

The Italian Left is irremediably unlovable. Its arrogant, presumptuous sense of moral superiority makes it unbearable, because it regards everyone else as brainless idiots incapable of any critical ability whatsoever. This complete lack of humility prevents it from being sufficiently self-critical to admit its own errors, and thus remedy them. How can anyone who won't admit he is ill get treatment? The Left's real problem lies in its inability to relate or adapt to reality, which it always filters through its own ideological screen. It's no use proving that Mr. B. is a crook. That won't stop people voting for him, but the Left has yet to figure this out.

Patrizio Giulioni

These letters, published in 2009 and 2010 on my online forum, "Italians,"[6] reveal a widespread conviction. The Italian Left is often incomprehensible, even to those who dislike Mr. B. and do not vote for him. It proposes confused solutions to complex problems with a contrite expression. Italy would prefer simple solutions presented with a smile. Perhaps Margaret Thatcher's acronym, coined to underline her indispensability—T.I.N.A., for There Is No Alternative—is excessive in an Italian context, but clearly Mr. B. is not burdened with a surfeit of competition.

As we have seen, he has managed to pass himself off as the "Can-Do Man." Do well, do badly, now and again do for his own benefit. But do, or at least appear to be doing. Ministers are expected to mention the government's laws, reforms, and other initiatives on every possible occasion. Minister Mariastella Gelmini gave *Il Giornale* newspaper a full list, after pointing out that Silvio Berlusconi "is a talent scout who promotes those who deserve promotion. In contrast, the Left never has any new faces."[7]

- getting public accounts under control

- cracking down on illegal immigration

- the Prisons Plan and the Homes Plan

- abolishing the ICI property tax on first homes

- a return to nuclear power

- the new traffic code

- restarting public works

- university reform

- school reform

- reform of public-sector employment

- reducing regional healthcare expenditure

- combating organized crime

- post-earthquake reconstruction in Abruzzo

- garbage emergency in Campania

- rescuing Alitalia

Let's just put into perspective these declarations by a serving minister with plenty of practice at simplifying, emphasizing, and omitting. We should bear in mind that some of these results are partial (Abruzzo), temporary (garbage in Naples), controversial (school reform), or in the future (prisons, homes, nuclear power, universities), while others have been achieved at the taxpayers' expense (Alitalia), or at the cost of human suffering and international incomprehension (illegal immigration). Nevertheless, some successes are undeniable, such as reining in public spending, praised by *The Economist,* among others, or the body blows delivered to organized crime.[8]

What about the difficulties and failures? Those are attributable to others: the bureaucrats, the magistrates, the mysterious "strong powers," or the world economy. The major television newscasts convince the masses, while the Five Million Club of well-informed Italians is dealt with by university professor–ministers like Renato Brunetta and

Giulio Tremonti. "In Italy," explained Tremonti, "we have accumulated a huge quantity of pointless rules, which create bottlenecks. Their architecture is dominated by the ideology of a perfect society, perfect rights, and perfect duties. That's not the way it is with the economic giants we compete against around the world."[9] It's an apology of imperfection, a raw material in which Italy abounds.

Then there is Tremonti's political underpinning, the Northern League, a local, populist, and popular movement that thrives on its opponents' shortcomings.

"Popular" is a compliment; "populist" is not an insult; and "local" is a statement of fact. In order to galvanize voters in the north, Umberto Bossi sometimes offends those elsewhere (at the Potato Fair in Lazzate on September 27, 2010: "*SPQR, Sono Porci Questi Romani* [These Romans Are Pigs]"). Yet this antagonism is the gas that fuels a nation whose engine is Siena's Palio horse race, as we will see. Rows die down, but the Northern League endures with its protests (at waste), proposals (fiscal federalism), and fantasies (independence for "Padania").

In the early 1990s, success came from reaction to the corrupt, inflexible party system, as did the overwhelming majorities in the election referendums, the Clean Hands investigations, and Berlusconi's Forza Italia party. Even today, with the Northern League a pillar of government, its members still look on parliamentary democracy with sarcastic skepticism. Which explains why they tolerate the U-turns, inconsistencies, and Lenin-style leadership of Umberto Bossi. As Roberto Maroni said, "Lenin knew what a party is: thousands of people to be motivated, one in charge, and the rest carrying out a project."

Bossi is shrewd. In the homeland of guile, he outcunnings them all. A lot of water has passed under Italy's bridges since *il Senatùr*, as Bossi is known, gave interviews while driving a rented Citroën on the A8 Milan-Lakes autostrada, looking at his interviewer and not the road (1992); or the day he took a stunned Johnny Grimond, *The Economist's* foreign editor, to see a rocket labeled "Padania" rising out of a swamp representing Italy (1997). "I show you the rocket!" is a phrase that even today has resonance in *The Economist* newsroom.[10]

A lot of water, as we were saying, and Northern League water is less murky than others. Anyone on the bridge, trying to work out which way the river is going, needs to understand this, instead of just criticizing the inconsistencies, the cringe-inducing comments, or the flamboyant ally he pushed into the prime minister's office and kept there.

Practical, popular, swift, and celebrated: four adjectives that the Italian Left has difficulty grasping, and that Mr. B. handles like a juggler. Pietrangelo Buttafuoco maintains, "The only one who will be included in the chapter of history that relates the Italy of our day is Silvio Berlusconi, with all his extravagances, eccentricities, and subversions."[11] The claim needs to be trimmed of the provocative Futurism that Italy's Right uses to gloss over the problems of our democracy, but it does contain an insight. Free of convictions or conventions, with plenty of enthusiasm and few scruples, mixing public instruments with private interests, Mr. B. looks more modern than his opponents.

When he realized that the rules-obsessed Right so dear to Indro Montanelli was destined to remain in the minority, he dreamed up another Right: practical, populist, muscular, aspirational, realist, and relativist. A home for exiled Socialists, born-again Christian Democrats, red-haters, ex-Communists, former Fascists, post-Fascists, idealists, cynics, politicos with no past, and those under judicial investigation. Silvio's majority embraced the far Right, the odd liberal, what remains of the Republicans, Sicilian independence campaigners, and north Italian separatists.

The result is a party with no congresses, a single leader, and one true ally (the Northern League) that has had several names in seventeen years: Forza Italia, Pole of Freedoms, House of Freedoms, and, finally, having absorbed the National Alliance, People of Freedom. Electoral laws have done the rest. The one currently in force, as we know, gives a majority in Parliament to the largest, best-organized minority. Guess what that is, and who put it together.

Meanwhile, the opposition is a swarm of names, abbreviations, and formations. The main one is the Democratic Party (PD) led by Pier Luigi Bersani, tempted by the new Olive Tree Alliance with Massimo D'Alema and challenged by Walter Veltroni's old Olive Tree Alliance. Among its former names are The Thing, Oak Tree, The Thing 2, Democratic Party of the Left, Democrats of the Left, Alliance for Democracy, Alliance of Progressives, Great Democratic Alliance, Federation for the Olive Tree, Democrats for the Olive Tree, and more besides, now forgotten. Following on are Antonio Di Pietro's Italy of Values (IDV), Beppe Grillo's Five Star Movement, Nichi Vendola's Left, Ecology, and Freedom, Francesco Rutelli's Alliance for Italy (API), Radicals, Socialists, and a great gaggle of nominally Communist movements that glory in their own anachronistic nature. Provisional positions are occupied by Pier Ferdinando Casini's Center Union and Future and Freedom for Italy (FLI), founded by the leader of the Chamber of Deputies, Gianfranco Fini.

Faced with all this, voters feel lost, like shoppers in a vast mall with no brands, labels, or counter staff. Some distractedly pick up one or two items and then give up. Soon, everyone is heading for the exit, where a short, well-dressed man is waiting for them with a smile. He stands on the doorstep all day long, selling the same product. But he explains, simplifies, entertains, reassures, and lets you have a discount.

Many say, "Why not?"

CHAPTER TEN

The Palio Factor

T he satisfaction of victory is as nothing compared to the joy of knowing your rival has lost.

This is not a quotation from a Renaissance historian, but it does sum up an ancient, and very modern, Italian attitude. In German, *schadenfreude* is gloating over the misfortunes of others, an unmentionable, private emotion. Italian euphoria at an adversary's failure is public, acceptable, and accepted. Since it doesn't have a name yet, we'll call it the Palio Factor.

Winning matters in Siena's Palio horse race, but equally—perhaps more—important is that your rival should lose. Inter-*contrada* (district) animosity is reciprocal, and reciprocally necessary. If the Eagle detests the Panther, the Panther despises the Eagle. The Porcupine can't stand the She-Wolf so the She-Wolf won't tolerate the Porcupine. The Owl is hostile to the Unicorn, which means the Unicorn will be the Owl's enemy.[1] The pairings aren't permanent, but they are consolidated. Loathing is a tango you can't dance alone.

The current star of the Palio is a jockey nicknamed Trecciolino (Little Tress), perhaps not the most appropriate name to introduce an analogy with the follicularly challenged *Cavaliere* ("The Knight," Berlusconi's nickname). Trecciolino, whose real name is Luigi Bruschelli, has won the Palio twelve times, only two times fewer than the legendary Aceto (Vinegar, Andrea De Gortes), and three wins shy of Bastiancino (Little Contrarian, Mattia Mancini), who won fifteen races in the second half of the eighteenth century. Mr. B.'s tally is still only three general elections, but he can also point to successes in administrative and European elections, as well as referenda. It's a track record that withstands comparison with the best.

For sixteen years, every vote has been about him. Italians know this and complain, but at heart they are not that sorry. From Savona to Siracusa, we all stick up for our political contrada. Loyalty to a man and a flag are mirror images of hostility to the opposing flag and whoever is carrying it. This is much more gut feeling than reasoned reflection. You don't support a contrada, they say in Siena—you belong to it.

✿

Passion and aversion for Silvio Berlusconi, as we have tried to demonstrate in this book, are often pre-political sentiments. Mr. B. embodies and evokes characteristics that some Italians find reassuring and others find intolerable, perhaps because they possess some of them. But those who find them reassuring find it intolerable that others should find them intolerable. They declare a silent war that fills their lives.

As we have seen, the Italian Left has a sensational knack for looking irritatingly antiquated. Silvio spotted this and he assiduously massages the sentiment. The video speech in which he "took the field" is repeated today with few variations.

> The parties of the Italian Left claim they have changed,
> and are now Liberal Democrats. But it's not true. Their
> people are still the same, their mentality, their culture,
> their deepest convictions, and their behavior are still the
> same. (January 26, 1994)
>
> The Left has been saying it has changed for years.
> But it's not true. Its people are still the same, and
> their behavior is still the same. And the allies they
> have chosen are even worse than they are. They have
> put together a terrifying hodgepodge that sees them
> marching arm in arm with, or rather handcuffed to, the
> paladin of hard-line legalism [former public prosecutor

and protagonist of Operation Clean Hands, now leader of the Italy of Values party, Antonio di Pietro. —Ed.]. (March 20, 2010)

I listened to what I had to say sixteen years ago about the Left. It's still the same Left it has always been. . . . In all these years, the Left has remained tied to its past. It has the same men, even the same offices, the same ideologies, the same arrogance, the same domineering attitude, and the same anything but democratic convictions.[2] (October 3, 2010)

Why does Mr. B. refer to a failed ideology like communism on all possible—and many improbable—occasions?[3] Because for a long time, communism was Italy's bogeyman. Often, anti-communism became a family tradition. It's not unusual to hear a twenty-year-old, born after the Berlin Wall came down, declaring "I will never vote for the Communists!" Unfamiliar with them when they were around, and uninformed now that they are no more. But afraid to catch communism, as if it were contagious.

Most Italians don't like the word. It has the taste of historic failure and mandatory altruism, which fly in the face of all Italy's national instincts. Mr. B. knows this, and plays on it. He performed an impressive cadenza on the theme during a rally at Cinisello Balsamo on June 19, 2009, on the eve of the second round of the Milan provincial elections: "You are still, today as ever, just sad Communists."[4]

Anti-communism is not the only tool with which Mr. B. tickles Italians' sectarianism. He has identified an antagonist for every section of the electorate, turning it into an attractive target for hostility. He has pointed the finger at anticlericalists for Catholics, moralists for the immoral, magistrates for those on trial, anti-Fascists for the post-Fascists, Second World War partisans for the revisionists, environmentalists for construction magnates, animal rights activists for the hunting lobby, tax inspectors for tax evaders, and his foreign critics for xenophobes. He didn't even have to indicate southern Italians to northerners, or northerners to people from the south. The Northern League and Mr. B.'s Sicilian allies took care of that.

Silvio knows how to urbanely set one group against another, and since there are plenty of groups, he can carry on playing the game as long as he likes. "We will never do anything like that to you. We are free, we are liberal in spirit. We will let you express your views!" he shouted at protesters in Milan's Piazza Duomo, just before he was wounded by a mentally disturbed assailant. "That's why we have to oppose you! Because you want to turn Italy into a shouting match in the street! . . . Don't trust people who are always like that. People who can't make fun of themselves, are always sore at something, never smile, and don't know how to love their neighbor!"[5]

Love against hate. Right against Left. Us against you. Me against everyone else. The Siena Palio is held twice a year; Silvio's is never-ending. Italy's contrade are exhausted, but they can always find the strength to squabble.

Our national story is an anthology of firmly rooted rivalries. Sport has provided Bartali/Coppi from cycling; Inter/Juventus, Rivera/Mazzola, and Rossi/Biaggi from soccer. Movies gave us star rivalries like Lollobrigida/Loren, and character conflicts like Peppone/Don Camillo. Television hosts (Baudo/Bongiorno), singers (Morandi/Villa, Ligabue/Vasco), motoring (Vespa/Lambretta, Lancia/Alfa), and fashion (Armani/Valentino) have all contributed. Geography and history have made Italy a dual system of rival towns: Milan/Turin, Trieste/Udine, Verona/Brescia, Bologna/Modena, Crema/Cremona, Pisa/Livorno, Florence/Siena, Naples/Salerno, Palermo/Catania, Bari/Lecce, Catanzaro/Reggio Calabria, and Cagliari/Sassari. Where there is no external enemy, the town splits in two. At microscopic Fucecchio, in the province of Florence, the *ingiuesi* from the lower part of the village constantly bickered with the *insuesi* from the upper area. Indro Montanelli, who was born in Fucecchio, used to amuse listeners by recalling how unions between an ingiuese and an insuese were regarded as mixed marriages.

Proximity doesn't ease hostility; it intensifies hostility. It's hard to get worked up about people on the other side of the planet, but it's great fun to compete with someone who lives on the other side of the street. As Silvio has figured out. Which is why he looks for enemies everywhere, and poses as a rival at all times. There are individuals, and political groupings, that have made anti-Berlusconism their raison d'être, something that Mr. B. has encouraged while pretending to be hurt about it. It is no coincidence that Fausto Bertinotti (the communist!) used to be on television all the time,[6] or that Antonio Di Pietro (the ruthless legalist!) still is.

The Center-Left's candidate in the 2008 elections, Walter Veltroni, realized this, but then overreacted, refusing even to pronounce the name "Berlusconi" and referring instead to "the principal exponent of the opposing formation." The periphrasis was so artificial that it revealed what lay behind it: a hostility similar to that nursed by his predecessors.

Italy's two-coalition system does not pit two programs or two worldviews against each other, as it does in other democracies. We have two opposing aversions, which are not Berlusconism and anti-Berlusconism, as some would have us believe. What we have is anti-Berlusconism and a reaction to it. Mr. B.'s supporters are first and foremost opponents of his opponents. The Right's greatest joy is watching the Left lose.

If the Right happens to win as well, so much the better.

A nation as conservative as Italy craves revolutionary words to ease its conscience, and then it's business as usual. The Right had this worked out long ago, but that particular idea has yet to sink in with the Left.

In his book *La sfida* [The Challenge], the left-wing mayor of Turin, Sergio Chiamparino, writes, "The leaders of the Right were able to present themselves as the force of protest against the system. They are the ones storming the Winter Palace. And we are the czar, defending privilege and piling furniture against the door in a last desperate attempt to stop them."[7]

The quotation reveals Chiamparino's age—many younger Italians might assume that the Winter Palace is where Mr. B. unwinds during the Christmas holidays—but it does pinpoint the problem. Against all evidence, Silvio Berlusconi and Umberto Bossi manage to pass themselves off as devil-may-care Futurists. The Left is forced to extemporize critiques of other people's art. In the long run, this is boring.

If we can flit from art to biology this resembles a form of parasitism, a relationship between two species that leads to the physical decline of one, while the other gains only benefits. It is not enough not to mention your opponent, as we have seen. You need to convince people that they can live without him.

Being new is not enough: You have to look new. In 1990s Britain, Tony Blair's Labour defeated the Conservatives when they started to treat Margaret Thatcher as an amusing museum piece. David Cameron's Conservatives paved the way for their own election win in 2010 by returning the compliment: We are the new; you have already had your turn. Thanks and good-bye.

There's no point in reminding Mr. B. of his broken election pledges. He'll just say that they didn't let him keep them, pointing to mistakes by the party,[8] treacherous opponents, diabolical regulations, the international economic situation, and unfavorable alignment of the stars. It would be better for the opposition to offer voters a detailed counterproposal, a precise idea of Italy, an achievable dream.

The nation is like a train that has stopped in the middle of the countryside. The driver is arguing with the guard while the passengers look on, rooting for one or the other.

The 150th anniversary of Italy's unity (1861–2011) will play itself out amid the squabbles of the gray-heads and the yawns of those Italians who still have dark hair. Let's focus on 2020. It's an aesthetically pleasing number and in Italy these things matter.

Mr. B. will be a fading memory by then, a nightmare for some, regretted by others. He should be a warning to all. As Gian Piero Alloisio pointed out, what counts isn't Berlusconi in himself, but Berlusconi in us.[9] Silvio spotted this, too: "Why do my fellow citizens appreciate me in such numbers? Because deep down, most Italians want to be like me."[10]

Silvio certainly got a bargain. For us, it wasn't such a good deal.

The Ruby Factor

I taly is at the mercy of an 18-year-old Moroccan and a dental hygienist. That's Italy, as in founders of the European Union and the world's seventh-largest economy. We may not like it, but Arcore party queens Ruby Heartstealer and Nicole Minetti are emblematic of our country. Italy is celebrating its 150th birthday. Father of the Nation Camillo Benso, Count of Cavour, couldn't have foreseen this.

It would be superfluous to describe in detail the lifestyle that Signora Veronica—it's always the wives—warned us about.[1] Newspapers and newscasts have done it for us, with the glorious exception of RAI TV's TG1, which on the day the storm broke led with "Tunisia turns over a new leaf."

("At least they did," commented one appalled, but encouragingly flippant reader.)

What we need to realize, regardless of our views on the methods of investigation, is the sheer enormity of it all. The loud debate on television is a smokescreen clouding the heart of the matter, which is this: Depressingly, the head of government of a major western power is facing charges of underage prostitution. But Mr. B. says he's being persecuted and hates people judging him. On several occasions, he has opined that "magistrates are the cancer of Italian democracy."[2]

Complicated? "Oh, yes," as we polyglots in Milan like to say. The picture that emerged from phone taps, in the public domain once the case file was forwarded to the appropriate committee in the Chamber of Deputies,[3] reveals more than just a jaw-dropping lifestyle (unless your jaw stays firmly in place for other reasons). It involves Italian institutions, elected bodies, and state services—for example, the questionable use of police escorts.

The papers are not interested in this as celebrity gossip, whatever some biased or superficial observers may claim. They're talking about a man who should be leading us, but instead is setting a catastrophic example. Luckily, younger Italians have already put this behind them. For the young, the Berlusconi that older Italians get worked up about is yesterday's news.

"Moralists!" cry those with no morals of their own. "What about Bill Clinton and Monica Lewinsky?" add the uninformed, in search of excuses. Well, Clinton didn't object to going on trial,[4] and there's a difference between an occasional lover and industrial-scale debauchery. We should stop trying to draw improbable analogies and pose the question a visitor from outer space might ask: "What is happening to Italy, and to those Italians who are tempted yet again to sweep it all under the carpet?"

Making light of everything makes the future seem a long way off. But another day inexorably arrives, unless the Kaiser Chiefs were right when they sang: "Due to lack of interest / Tomorrow is canceled."[5] The song was called "Ruby." Let's hope it was just a coincidence.

The Left in Italy has only ever judged Silvio Berlusconi; it has never attempted to explain him. Neither has the Right, having been too busy defending or applauding him. Recent revelations, however, demand a little intellectual honesty. When the *Financial Times*, perhaps Europe's most influential daily newspaper, talks about "a huge shame for Italy,"[6] we cannot ignore it.

The events described are serious; the picture painted disturbs. This has nothing to do with the spectacular inconsistencies between a leader's personal life and his public manifesto. It's a question of conscience (and a question for the Catholic Church, if it's interested). Nor is this a political verdict. That will come from the polling booths. (We saw the first signs in the May 2011 administrative elections.) No, these are serious, precisely formulated charges that an organization was set up for the purpose of prostitution using the staff, premises, television channels, and protection services of the head of government. The allegation is chilling, and it should be proved or disproved.

If the charge is unfounded, the public prosecutors will have to face the music. Silvio Berlusconi will be able to claim he is a victim of persecution, and we will believe him. But if it is true, the defendants—and their reputations—will pay the price. One way or another, someone has to be called to account. This time, not knowing is a price we cannot afford to pay. Flabbergasted foreign observers expect to know, as do the equally severe young commentators who share our homes with us. What is happening to us? We owe the new generation of Italians, to whom this book is addressed, some sort of answer.

"The world's seventh-largest economy needs reform," wrote the *Financial Times*. "One in four youths is unemployed; growth is less than anemic; foreign investment is falling; national debt has hit €1,800bn. The cancer of organized crime needs excising. The list goes on," the *FT* mused. "Yet instead of solutions to these problems, the country is likely to be treated to another installment of Berlusconi versus the judiciary."[7]

This is the spectacle that must be averted. We've had enough of it it. In recent months, there has been an atmosphere of shell-shocked burn-out that transcends ideologies and party lines. We know the Right's suspicions about the courts, and the way impotent sections of the Left place their hopes in the legal system. But if you're going to keep complaining about the umpire, you might as well quit the ball game. Italy's game is called democracy. We have to play and win, particularly on the 150th anniversary of the country's unification (1861–2011). Our other option is to turn a birthday into a funeral. Not a great idea.

Silvio Berlusconi will have to be enormously courageous, because the charges themselves are enormous, but this time, there is no hiding place—for him or for us. For years, Silvio has been our good buddy. He has forgiven us, egged us on, absolved us, justified us, built up our hopes, and kept up our spirits. But there is a fine line between complicity and embarrassment, and another deeper divide that separates embarrassment from disgust. The line has been crossed. In a democracy, the divide should never be overstepped. Because it is humiliating, it is dangerous, and the *Financial Times* is right. Italy deserves better.

There are deferential commentators and independent ones. What can we say to the former? Perhaps: "What does the Boss have to do before you will say or write not a criticism—perish the thought!— but perhaps as a doubt, a perplexity, or even an objection?"

You get the impression that the bunga-bunga parties are Berlusconi's "Ruby-con." Once crossed, there is no return. We probably won't slide into authoritarianism:

Italians are too lazy for that sort of thing. This is politics as pop art. Creativity, skimpily clad, has taken over. Comedian Antonio Albanese expressed the sentiment in the screen role of sleazy, lexically adventurous politico Cetto La Qualunque: "Reality outstrips us consideratiously."[8]

And what can we say to the independent commentators? Concentrating on form while ignoring substance is a mistake. Are the magistrates going a tad too far? Have they overstepped bounds, or overreached? No one in London or Berlin cares whether jurisdiction falls to the public prosecutor's office in Milan or to the one in Monza. They want to know whether an important ally has the debauchery-drenched and supplicant-strewn lifestyle of a late-empire satrap or not. It's not that European governments are moralistic, but the lifestyle in question leaves their ally open to blackmail.

The same is true of international public opinion. Italians abroad know what is going on. Ask them how humiliated they have been feeling in recent months, after years of embarrassment. In British banks, French corporations, American universities, and German consulates, people are smiling and/or laughing at us, depending on the occasion and how sadistic the snickerer is. I would ask the professional face-savers: Why do you want the media to keep quiet about all this? Why don't you tell him, and them, to stop doing it? Have you any idea what would happen if the photos and videos were to get out, as some fear, others hope, and paparazzo Fabrizio Corona has announced?[9] Italy would be a caricature of a western country, if we aren't a joke already.

In 2010 and 2011, I visited a large number of schools and met thousands of students. It had been a long time, and I enjoyed the experience. Young people always give us more than we give them. As I looked at the oldest of those students—young Italians born in 1992—they reminded me of budding seafarers. Their ship is casting off, the sea is rough, and we can only hope we have taught them what they need to know. When the storms hit, we won't necessarily be there.

Elisa, a teacher from Padua, wrote to my "Italians" forum on Corriere.it, "These youngsters need adults who can convince them to dream, because their wings are strong, even though they don't seem to want to fly." I would add that if we can't inspire, we could at least refrain from confusing them with bad examples. Italy's bright-eyed 18-year-old girls ought to be in class with boys their own age, not selling dreams, and other things, for the nocturnal amusement of rich old men.

The public, torn between curiosity and irritation, asks how, where, how much? Magistrates want to know who and when. Yet the sixth question—why?—is never posed.

Why does Mr. B. behave this way? Why does such an important man—a head of government, no less—surround himself with courtiers and handmaids? The simple answer might be because he likes it that way. Not so much the sex, which at a certain age presents mountain-high challenges, as approval and her three sisters, admiration, adulation, and adoration.

The choreography described by party attendees is similar in some respects to other situations the host enjoys: conferences with adoring young female supporters, television award presentations, Brazilian nights, Russian dachas, Sardinian villas, and ceremonies at provincial universities near Milan. At times, Mr. B's narcissism is weapons-grade intense. He wants to be applauded and appreciated. It's one of the reasons he hates journalists, apart from his pet in-house scribes. Aggressive questions suggest he is not loved. And that would never do.

In Mr. B, our national penchant for showing off, the instinct that drives us to want to make a *bella figura* (good impression), becomes incandescent and generates energy. Enough energy to go without sleep, caution, or common sense. Energy that prompts him to use his television stations as bait and reward. Energy that induces him to promote, protect, and include young women on election lists on aesthetic or sexual grounds, defending them beyond all semblance of logic. It's also the energy that enables Giampaolo Pansa to ignore the grotesque aspects of the story in *Libero* newspaper. After a long, absolutory introduction, he calls it "the ecstasy of a trash film director discovering the heirs of [B-movie stars from the 1970s—Ed.] Bombolo, Alvaro

Vitali, and the various Ubaldas who are always hot for it, dressed as nurses, teachers, and policewomen."[10]

The single man in a nightclub, who features in so many films and so much fiction, is looking for the same thing. The carefully staged pretend parties, the compliments, the flattery, the parody of seduction, the predictable temptation, and paying for the illusion of allure are human foibles, and all too Italian, but that's no excuse, given the circumstances, positions, and ages, among other things, of the women involved. Yet there is something familiar about this frenetic quest for approval, whose symptoms—long known in Mr. B.'s business circles and political party, where he is, respectively, "the doctor" and "the president"—became public knowledge two years ago. Judges and journalists weren't responsible. The blame lies with Mr. B.'s spectacular lack of caution.

Attending the 18th birthday party of Noemi Letizia on the outskirts of Naples—an incident we have already mentioned—was a sublime piece of showing off. What Italy's richest, most powerful man was after that evening was the look of astonishment in the guests' eyes. On other occasions, he has made guests at his Arcore, Palazzo Grazioli, and Villa Certosa homes watch videos of his meetings with the world's great and good. More showing off. Some people need an audience. If they can't find one, they buy one.

There's a touch of Tiberius (as described by Roman historian Suetonius),[11] and a helping of Hugh Hefner (immortalized by *Playboy*), in all this. Empires decline in a similar way, crumbling amidst parties, indulgence, and attempts to halt the clock with tricks that time has taught us to recognize. Families, interests, and professional successes are no longer enough. Sycophants, female fans and singers are required, as well as scenery both spectacular and saddening, mainly because it is designed to dispel sadness.

Mr. B. is a lonely man. He'll realize this as soon as he loses power. Suddenly, prices will rise and friends will disappear. Those who care about him should tell him this, but perhaps it's too late.

Milan, Modena, Genoa, Turin, Padua, Pavia, Aosta, Marsala, Palermo, Cagliari, Nuoro, Sassari, Florence, Perugia, or Bergamo. Presenting a book on Berlusconi to the public means listening to opinions about Berlusconi. And when there aren't any opinions, there are inquisitive looks, strained smiles, startled eyes, and open mouths. Every time, there's a bit of everything, and something to learn. It has not been so much the critics as Mr. B.'s defenders who have impressed me, especially the ones who are longer in the tooth. Many older Italians exhibit a determination to protect reminiscent of a veteran offensive line. Mr. B. is their quarterback, and no one is going to touch him.

In Nuoro, an 80-year-old lady marched up to me while I was having lunch, "Mind what you say about Berlusconi tonight!" It wasn't so much a threat as an over-assertive entreaty, with the subtext, "Don't disappoint me. Don't tell me that those things were going on in those houses on those nights!" I could have told her that we were in the hometown of legal scholar Salvatore Satta, and that for her hero, and our prime minister, "The Day of Judgment"[12] was nigh. I didn't, because I respect—and fear—gray panthers.

Question: Why do people who for decades have preached and practiced moderation defend the bungabunga lifestyle? Why do gentlemen beyond reproach, who have absolutely nothing in common with sleazy TV agent Lele Mora, stand up for a man who keeps such dubious company? Why do they shut their eyes to Mr. B.'s spectacular serial inconsistencies? Don't they know? Do they perhaps not want to know?

The answer, I believe, is in three parts.

An entire generation sincerely feared the coming of communism, when the communists were real. The sentiment is too deep-rooted to eliminate. Over the years, it has been fed by irritation at sham-progressive hypocrisy, trade union-linked arrogance, anti-American fanaticism, and a degree of judicial mission creep. For these Italians, Berlusconi is the man who led the Right to victory and condemned the Left to defeat. Nothing else matters, or matters quite as much.

Spectacular excess, heart-melting self-regard, and jaw-dropping attacks of amnesia. Mr. B. embodies a type Italians born in the 1920s and 1930s know well. He is the lovable 1960s reprobate who drove around in a sports car, put drinks for everyone on his tab, and hit on the woman who brought them. Italians close an indulgent eye to Silvio's intemperances. When at the height of the scandal, he blurted out "I'm having fun," few—apart from Italy's 80-year-olds—realized he was telling the truth.

Finally, there's repression. The charges are serious, the details toe curling. The stories going around are humiliating, their implications traumatic. With the passing years, our brain learns to erase bad memories and unwelcome information. It's a survival mechanism. And that's what the gray panthers do. They forget, or watch RAI TG1 news.

There is a dark, conniving side to the Italian character, as the subtitle of Ermanno Rea's book, *La fabbrica dell'obbedienza* [The Obedience Factory],[13] reminds us. Yet we continue to ignore it. No one wants a North African–style uprising—heaven forfend—but a touch of healthy skepticism wouldn't hurt. Many of us, however, lap it all up. Including the government press, a contradiction in terms that fails to faze our assorted liberals, but leaves any non-Italian observer openmouthed.

Three women journalists from RAI 5 came to see me. Their program is called *La Banda del Book* [The Book Gang]. The gang visits the victim's home and goes through his or her library. As they were leaving, the gangsters asked me to choose one of three literary endings. I chose one from Mark Twain. His *Freedom of the Press* concludes: "We all do no end of feeling, and we mistake it for thinking. And out of it we get an aggregation which we consider a boon. Its name is Public Opinion. It is held in reverence. It settles everything. Some think it is the voice of God."[14]

A brilliant insight from Mark Twain, a.k.a. Samuel Langhorne Clemens (1835–1910). We feel with our guts and think with our heads. Feeling is immediate, but thinking takes time. People have neither the time nor the inclination to find out the facts and draw conclusions. In any democracy, not just Italy. The sheer mass of information is exhausting and irritating, but many of us don't want to be disturbed.

Politicians have figured this out. They use advertising's topics, methods, and timing, giving us small doses of gratifying information at the right moment. American candidates bankrupt themselves to buy air time. British and German politicians vie for the backing of the tabloid press. Mr. B. maintains consensus through the simplifications that the media (which he owns and controls) circulate beyond the Five Million Club, the Italians who are well informed and, as we saw in "The Truman Factor," talk a lot but count for much less.

The conflict of interest is canceled out by the vote! A seductive, but erroneous, assertion because the vote can be—and in fact, is—influenced by the conflict of interest. *The final judge is the people!* It sounds good, but that's not what the Italian constitution says when it lays down the separation of powers. *Private life is sacred!* Not always. We have to assess a leader's integrity, reliability, honesty, and responsibility. *I'm paying you. You should be backing me up!* It sounds logical, but it isn't. For example, journalists and A.C. Milan soccer players have other jobs to do.

Those who listen fall in love with the exclamation points. Those who reflect arrive at the subsequent objections. But there isn't much time to think in our complicated, interconnected lives. There's enough time to feel, though. Get the timing right, and you will be able to convince us. We are overinformed, yet misinformed, cynical, ingenuous, defenseless, and presumptuous. We are public opinion. We are Italy's articulate gut.

The circus is open, the show has begun, the world is laughing, and we—I fear—are the clowns. The sleek blue sky, the green of the burgeoning leaves, and the white antennas of TV vans from five continents salute Milan's judicial spring. Yet the seven minutes that failed to shake the world left a bitter taste as the fast-track procedure of Silvio Berlusconi's hearing on charges of underage prostitution and abuse of power sputtered to a swift conclusion.[15] The legitimate international attention was widely expected. If the same charges were brought against any other western head of government, there would be a comparable mobilization of the press. The question remains: Why is it always us?

Paula, the Argentine journalist who thought she had seen it all in terms of populism, street politics, and political

coiffure, can only smile. Emma from Australia is astonished by the impression of talk-show host Bruno Vespa on
the satirical TV show *Striscia la notizia* because she has
never seen the original. Leah from Canada mumbles, "But
I thought it was a real trial!" Barbara Serra looks regal in
cobalt blue as she asks me live on Al Jazeera, "How do you
explain 'bunga bunga' to the Arab world?" "'Bunga bunga'
is the sound tens of millions of disbelieving Italian heads
make as they're being struck against the wall," I reply.

Why is it always us, frozen for almost eighteen years in
the same snapshot of Italy? Mr. B. against the magistrates
with the Palace of Justice in the background, and a public
that takes sides first and worries about the facts later. The
world rises up, gets excited, changes, erupts, and—now and
again—becomes a better place. And we're still here, unrav-
eling the dreary intrigues of a crumbling empire.

The press has to use the court's rear entrance on Via
San Barnaba. To get there from Corso di Porta Vittoria
you have to go along Via Freguglia, the street of cappuc-
cinos, duty stamps, long waits, and sighs of relief. Young
lawyers exchange greetings as they go about their daily
business. Like hospitals, palaces of justice swarm with
worried humanity and tired professionals. Inside, Milan's
courthouse has always reminded me of a Balkan university:
a muddle of skills, poor maintenance, high passions, exigu-
ous resources, great issues, and half-fulfilled dreams.

The courtroom borrowed from the first Assize Court
has seen dramatic trials unfold, from terrorism cases to the

healthcare horrors of the Santa Rita hospital.[16] The journalists, too, exchange greetings. There are plenty of us,
some carrying a few more kilograms and with a few more
books published, hair graying if we still have any. We are
the veterans of an unchanging Italy, witnesses under police
surveillance banned from using cell phones. The cages for
the defendants have been draped demurely in white cloths.
Here and there, the cloths part to reveal the metal under-
neath. Budget cuts have produced a surreal effect, like an
abstract sculpture by Lucio Fontana.

Prosecutor Ilda Boccassini comes in, a star despite her-
self in dark glasses and coral earrings. The panel of judges
enters. Everyone stands up to see three women surprised
by the unusually crowded courtroom. The name "Silvio
Berlusconi" rings out, followed by the adjective "absent,"
and the noun "default." Defense counsel Giorgio Perroni
speaks, standing in for Mr. B.'s regular lawyers, Piero Longo
and Niccolò Ghedini, for the trial. The lawyer defending
Karima El Mahroug speaks to say that Ruby Heartstealer
will not be appearing as co-plaintiff. End of story. Thank
you. Arrivederci.

Seven minutes. The amount of time the film censor
cut from Nanni Moretti's *The Caiman*, the title of a Russ
Meyer film, the length of Giuliano Ferrara's program
on RAIUno, and the correct duration of sexual congress
(according to the Internet).[17] The hearing, for formalities
only, is over. Ruby's lawyer, Paola Boccardi, speaks to a

wall of microphones as if she were the A.C. Milan manager, Leonardo, although he is usually in a better mood when facing the press. A few Berlusconi supporters and even fewer protesters wait outside, wearing bright colors and carrying placards for the cameras. They are just extras, too. Raging emotion for and against has given way to fatigue. The demonstrators are going through the motions now.

The journalists head back to their newsrooms, or to the nearest bar. Next time, perhaps the accused will turn up. A Turkish reporter clutching a notebook approaches and asks me what I think about it all. I reply, "Did you see that film where Bill Murray wakes up every morning and it's always the same day?[18] That's what Italy has been like for far too long. And, my friend from Istanbul, I can assure you that it's less fun than it looks from the outside."

How this book came about

he origins of this book lie in another, *La Testa degli italiani*, published in 2005 in Italy, in 2006 in the United States—under the title *La Bella Figura*—and since then in a dozen or so other countries. As I traveled around Europe and the rest of the globe, every time I met someone, I already knew what his or her first question would be, even before it was asked: "Berlusconi. Why?"

Sometimes the "why" would be outraged; on other occasions merely curious. Foreigners, no matter what their political leanings, simply couldn't, and still can't, understand why Mr. B. has been so successful for so long. They only know that he has dominated the Italian political scene and has been the principal—some would say the only—topic of conversation for seventeen years, since he first ventured into politics.

Why do non-Italians find it so hard to comprehend? Because if what goes on in the heads of Italians is mysterious, what they feel in their gut verges on the esoteric. Italian psychology is challenging; the gastroenterology can be distressing.

I realized this while I was writing for *The Economist* (1993-2003), the London *Sunday Times* (1993–1994), *TIME* magazine (2008), and the *New York Times* Syndicate (2007–2009). Further confirmation came in 2010, when the Italian Society of the London School of Economics invited me to discuss the topic. On that occasion—Thursday February 4, 2010, lecture room D202—I took as my title "Signor B.: An Italian Mirror?" and introduced my factor-based explanation, which was the jumping-off point for this book.

The same question—how could Italians possibly choose, support, and defend Berlusconi?—is posed, with impressive regularity, by the many journalists and writers I meet in Italy and abroad. Among them have been Anne Applebaum, who later featured our conversation in her column in the *Washington Post*; my former editor Bill Emmott, author of *Forza, Italia* (Rizzoli, 2010); the British historian David Gilmour, who addressed the subject in *The Pursuit of Italy* (Penguin, 2011); Matt Kaminski from the *Wall Street Journal*; Doyle McManus from the *Los Angeles Times*; colleagues from the BBC; and many others. I found them more curious than prejudiced. Unlike many Italian commentators, they sought sincerely to understand.

To be honest, I have found the same attitude in younger Italians, but in their case, not at public meetings. I have never contemplated talking about Silvio Berlusconi in schools. Some parents would be delighted, others furious. The younger Italians I am talking about are my son, his friends, my numerous nephews and nieces, my friends' children, and young people who visit "Italians," my forum on Corriere.it. Once we get onto the subject—and in Italy it is hard to avoid it—I realize that I am talking to new, curious people, keen to understand a man who, whether they like it or not, dominated the scene while they were growing up. There have been other important political figures since 1994, but if you think an eighteen-year-old remembers Romano Prodi's electoral hara-kiri in 1998, you are mistaken.

What else? It may be trite to say so, but posterity will hand down its sentence. This time, there is no statute of limitations. Silvio Berlusconi will be tried.

We have supplied as complete a range of sources as possible, including videos available on YouTube. The titles of individual clips, and the accompanying comments, do not represent the author's opinions.

The publisher is not responsible for the content of the websites mentioned, and apologizes if those sites should become inaccessible in the future.

Notes

CHAPTER ONE: THE HUMAN FACTOR

1. Fiorenza Sarzanini, "Autoscatti a Palazzo Grazioli. La serata delle tre ragazze" ["Photographing Yourself in Palazzo Grazioli—How Three Girls Spent Their Evening"], *Corriere della Sera*, June 22, 2009. From Corriere.it: http://bit.ly/boDIRo (in Italian).

2. Piero Gobetti, "Elogio della ghigliottina" ["In Praise of the Guillotine"], *La Rivoluzione Liberale*, year I, no. 34, November 23, 1922: "But Fascism was more than this: it was the nation's autobiography." (Source: http://www.erasmo.it/liberale/, digital archive of Centro Studi Piero Gobetti www.centrogobetti.it; both sites in Italian.)

3. Rome, media briefing for third Italy-Egypt summit, May 19, 2010.
   M.Ca., "E il premier scambia Google con Gogol" ["And the Prime Minister Confuses Google with Gogol"], *Corriere della Sera*, May 20, 2010.
   From Corriere.it: http://bit.ly/cozMQM (in Italian).

4. Author's own information.

5. Cáceres, Spain, meeting of European foreign ministers, February 8, 2002. From Repubblica.it: http://bit.ly/diVtqz (in Italian).

Strasbourg, presentation of Italy's six-month presidency of the Council of the European Union, July 2, 2003. From YouTube: http://bit.ly/aNDovz (in Italian).

Porto Rotondo, private visit by Tony Blair, August 16, 2004. From news section of Libero.it: http://bit.ly/borXrl (in Italian).

Paola Di Caro, "Calzoni di lino e bandana, Silvio spinge Tony al bagno di folla" ["Linen Shorts and Bandana for Silvio Taking Tony on Walkabout"], *Corriere della Sera*, August 17, 2004.

Bolzano, election rally with Michaela Biancofiore, May 29, 2005. From Corriere.it: http://bit.ly/amug4b (in Italian); from YouTube: http://bit.ly/9nHX9o (in Italian).

Parma, inauguration of the European Food Safety Authority, June 21, 2005. From Corriere.it: http://bit.ly/cAUdvh (in Italian); from YouTube/Blob: http://bit.ly/a2wwEr (in Italian).

Naples, election rally, March 26, 2006. From YouTube: http://bit.ly/9bN8GR (in Italian).

Rome, visit by Luis Inácio Lula da Silva, president of Brazil, November 11, 2008. From Sky Sport24 http://bit.ly/bgWjbY (in Italian).

Trieste, Italy-Germany summit, November 18, 2008. From Corriere.it: http://bit.ly/cE12Tq (in Italian).

Kehl, Germany, NATO summit, April 4, 2009. From Corriere.it: http://bit.ly/bZyOJa (in Italian); from Sky TG24: http://bit.ly/bj6FfC (in Italian).

London, G20, April 2, 2009. From Corriere.it: http://bit.ly/91HUKg (in Italian); from YouTube: http://bit.ly/aftjS1 (in Italian).

Rome, Senate, September 30, 2010. The New START 2 treaty was signed by Barack Obama and Dimitri Medvedev on April 8, 2010, in Prague. From YouTube: http://bit.ly/az3ccW (in Italian).

6. Nick Squires, "Silvio Berlusconi's Top 10 Gaffes and Pranks," *The Telegraph*, April 4, 2009.

From Time.com: http://bit.ly/c5QkOu.

From bbc.co.uk: http://bbc.in/bH8Izr.

7. From YouTube: http://bit.ly/dAmysc.

8. Teatro Eliseo, Nuoro, campaign for 2009 Sardinian regional elections, January 17, 2009.

Rome, Atreju 2010, September 12, 2010. From YouTube/Sky TG24: http://bit.ly/95kijY (no longer available).

Rome, outside Palazzo Grazioli, on the night of September 29 and 30, 2010. From YouTube/Repubblica TV: http://bit.ly/9IOZRA (in Italian).

9. Moscow, Italy-Russia summit, November 6, 2008. From YouTube: http://bit.ly/bNXrZv (in Italian).
10. New York, visit to the United States, meeting with business community, September 24, 2003.

   Gianluca Luzi, "Berlusconi, show a Wall Street: ho salvato l'Italia dai comunisti" ["Berlusconi Show on Wall Street—I Saved Italy from the Communists"], *La Repubblica*, September 25, 2003.

   Maria Latella, "Berlusconi invita Wall Street. In Italia meno comunisti" [Berlusconi Invites Wall Street—Fewer Communists in Italy], *Corriere della Sera*, September 25, 2003.
11. Rome, Italy-Albania summit, February 12, 2010.

   Vincenzo La Manna, "Berlusconi scherza con Berisha sulle «bellezze» dell'Albania" ["Berlusconi Jokes with Berisha about Albania's 'Beauties'"], *Il Giornale*, February 13, 2010.

   From YouTube: http://bit.ly/dqrzR1 (in Italian).
12. Milan, national festival of People of Freedom, October 3, 2010. From Sky TG24: http://bit.ly/cFybhU (in Italian).
13. Homes Plan, March 6, 2009. From Governo.it: http://bit.ly/9ZeHEt (in Italian).

   From ilsole24ore.com: http://bit.ly/a7osWo (in Italian).
14. Enrico Marro, "L'Italia delle case fantasma. Due milioni non denunciate" ["Italy's Phantom Homes—Two Million Unregistered Houses"], *Corriere della Sera*, July 24, 2010.
15. Massimiliano Scafi, "Ai giovani case con mutui inferiori agli affitti" ["Home Loan Payments Lower Than Rent for Young People"], *Il Giornale*, January 24, 2009.
16. Milan, national festival of People of Freedom, October 3, 2010. From YouTube/Sky TG24: http://bit.ly/ceJoZ3 (in Italian).
17. Natalia Ginzburg, *Le Piccole virtù*, Turin: Einaudi, 1962. Translated by Dick Davis as *The Little Virtues* (Manchester: Carcanet, 1985).
18. Edmondo Berselli, *Post italiani [Post-Italians]*, Milan: Mondadori, 2003, p. 3.
19. Andrea Romano, "Sottoculturali, tanto beati e incoscienti" ["Subcultural, So Happy, So Feckless"], *Il Sole 24 Ore*, July 25, 2010.
20. Renato Farina, "Berlusconi tale e quale. Vita, conquiste, battaglie e passioni di un uomo politico unico al mondo" ["The Real Berlusconi—Life, Conquests, and Passions of a Unique Politician"], *Libero*, 2009, no. 4, p. 73.
21. Francesco Verderami, "Giulio, ti dico: cambia metodo" ["I'm Telling You, Giulio, Change Your Approach"], *Corriere della Sera*, July 17, 2010.

CHAPTER TWO: THE DIVINE FACTOR

1. From Sky TG24: http://bit.ly/b6gG23 (in Italian).
2. Ernesto Galli della Loggia, *L'Identità italiana* [*The Italian Identity*], Bologna: Il Mulino, 1998, p. 47.
3. Emilia Costantini, "Ambra è una replicante: ecco le prove" ["Ambra is a Replicant—Here's Proof"], *Corriere della Sera*, December 10, 1994.
   From YouTube: http://bit.ly/cJscPZ (no longer available); http://bit.ly/9Q7GKE (no longer available).
   Paolo Conti, "Boncompagni: caso Ambra? Ragazzate" [Boncompagni Brushes off Ambragate as Kids' Prank], *Corriere della Sera*, February 2, 1994.
4. Pierluigi Battista, "Il caso. L'investitura del Cavaliere" ["Inquiry. The Knight's Investiture"], *La Stampa*, November 26, 1994.
5. Silvia Giacomoni, "Ma contro Dio più della DC ha potuto la tv" ["TV Did More Than DC Against God"], *La Repubblica*, August 30, 1994.
6. *Una Storia italiana* [*An Italian Story*], Mondadori Printing, 2001, election magazine. From www.pdl.it: http://bit.ly/8XmLzQ (in Italian).
   Giuliana Parotto, "Sacra Officina. La simbolica religiosa di Silvio Berlusconi" ["Holy Workshop—Silvio Berlusconi's Religious Symbolism"], Franco Angeli, Milan 2007.
   Riccardo Bruno, "Letture, orazioni e il «credo»: gli azzurri in seminario da Silvio" ["Readings, Prayers, and the Creed—Forza Italia's Seminary with Silvio"], *Corriere della Sera*, May 11, 2004.
   Luigi Frasca, "Sono il Gesù della politica, una vittima" ["I Am the Jesus Christ of Politics, a Victim"], *Il Tempo*, February 13, 2006.
7. Salvatore Dama, "Silvio cerca uomini di buona volontà" ["Silvio Seeks Men of Goodwill"], *Libero*, December 27, 2009.
   From Repubblica.it: http://bit.ly/ao1XOn (in Italian).
   The original Party of Love was founded on July 12, 1991, by supporters of Ilona Staller, better known as Cicciolina, a porn actress elected to the Chamber of Deputies on the Radical Party list in 1987. At the 1992 election, the party ran for the Chamber of Deputies in the nineteenth Lazio district (except Rieti), garnering 22,401 votes (0.6 percent). Election list leader Moana Pozzi received more votes (12,393) than future Center-Left prime ministerial candidate Francesco Rutelli. (Source: www.partitodellamore.it. In Italian.)
8. "Silvio, i candidati e il patto-preghiera" ["Silvio, the Candidates, and the Prayer-Pact"], *Corriere della Sera*, March 20, 2010. From YouTube/Sky TG24: http://bit.ly/dA3Doq (in Italian).
9. Gian Guido Vecchi, "L'arcivescovo: faccia chiarezza con i fatti"

["Archbishop Calls for Clarity about Deeds"], *Corriere della Sera*, June 21, 2009.

Antonio Sciortino, "Per una valutazione meno «disincantata»" ["Toward a Less 'Disenchanted' Assessment"], *Famiglia Cristiana*, June 25, 2009.

10. Angelus blessing at Apostolic Palace of Castel Gandolfo, August 22, 2010.

Aldo Cazzullo, "Il disagio dei cattolici" ["Catholics Uncomfortable"], *Corriere della Sera*, August 22, 2010.

11. On October 1 2010, the website of *L'Espresso* newsweekly posted an undated amateur video clip in which Silvio Berlusconi is telling a joke to a group of soldiers in Abruzzo. The joke involves Democratic Party leader Rosy Bindi and concludes with a blasphemous remark.

Reactions the following day included this call for caution from Monsignor Rino Fisichella: "At times like these, it is important to put things in context."

From *L'Espresso*: http://bit.ly/aBcqt6 (in Italian).

Giacomo Galeazzi, "La Chiesa critica il Premier: «Bestemmia insopportabile»" ["Church Slams Premier—'Intolerable Blasphemy'"], *La Stampa*, October 3, 2010.

12. Tommaso Labate, "Il premier «puttaniere»" ["The 'Whoremongering' Premier"], *Il Riformista*, March 26, 2009.

13. Mariastella Gelmini, "È il Pdl il partito più attento ai valori cattolici" ["PDL Is Party that Adheres Most to Catholic Values"], *Corriere della Sera*, August 23, 2010.

Emanuele Lauria, "Accuse disgustose e inaccettabili. La Chiesa non aiuta i fedeli in politica" ["Disgusting, Unacceptable Charges. Church Does Not Help Believers in Politics"], *La Repubblica*, August 25, 2010.

Martino Cervo, "Cattolici a sorpresa: un leader non si giudica solo dalla sua morale" ["Surprise as Catholics Claim Leader Should Not Be Judged By Morality"], *Libero*, July 26, 2009.

14. Gad Lerner, "La crociata di Cl contro i moralisti" ["Comunione e Liberazione's Crusade Against Moralists"], *La Repubblica*, August 28, 2010.

15. Segrate, Milan, April 17, 2010. From YouTube/Canale5: http://bit.ly/9lI5mr (in Italian).

16. Nicholas Farrell, "La sinistra critica Gheddafi ma non le moschee sotto casa" ["Left Criticizes Qaddafi But Not Local Mosques"], *Libero*, September 1, 2010.

17. Giuseppe De Rita, "Il cattolico post moderno e lo scarso peso in politica" ["The Political Irrelevance of the Postmodern Catholic"], *Corriere della Sera*, August 31, 2010.
18. From YouTube/RAIUno: http://bit.ly/b7Yhqs (no longer available).
19. Conversation with author.
20. Ferruccio Pinotti and Udo Gümpel, *L'Unto del Signore* [*The Lord's Anointed*], Milan: BUR Rizzoli, 2009, p. 278.
21. Gianni Baget Bozzo, "E ora è Berlusconi il vero leader morale dei cattolici" ["Berlusconi Is Now Catholics' True Moral Leader"], *Il Giornale*, February 10, 2009.
22. Aldo Cazzullo, "Il Cavaliere? Un dono di Dio all'Italia" ["Berlusconi? God's Gift to Italy"], *Corriere della Sera*, November 6, 2009.
    Grande Milano award, July 19, 2010. From YouTube: http://bit.ly/amUx9R (in Italian).

CHAPTER THREE: THE ROBINSON FACTOR

1. "Berlusconi: «L'inchiesta P3? Solo polvere. Basta con questo clima giacobino»" ["Berlusconi: 'P3 Inquiry Just Stirring Trouble. Enough of This Climate of Jacobinism'"], July 13, 2010. From Corriere.it: http://bit.ly/9zfQF4 (in Italian).
2. On-air phone call to the *Ballarò* program on RAITre, June 1, 2010. From YouTube: http://bit.ly/9S4Jg8 (no longer available).
    Rome, media briefing at Palazzo Chigi, February 17, 2004. From YouTube: http://bit.ly/d98REm (no longer available).
3. Jimmy Vescovi, "Tesi di laurea zoppe per un'Italia zoppa" ["Lame Degree Theses for a Lame Italy"], *Corriere della Sera*, October 7, 2010; "Italians": http://bit.ly/bwLxh2 (in Italian).
4. Giovanni Arpino, *Azzurro tenebra* [*Pitch Dark Blue*], Milan: BUR Rizzoli, 2010, p. 154.
5. Bill Emmott, *Forza, Italia* [*Go, Italy*], Milan: Rizzoli, 2010, p. 8.
6. Edward C. Banfield, *The Moral Basis of a Backward Society*, Chicago: University of Chicago, introduction.
7. Alexander Stille, *The Sack of Rome: Media + Money + Celebrity = Power = Silvio Berlusconi*, New York: Penguin, 2006, p. 267.
8. Conversation with the author and Johnny Grimond for *The Economist*, Palazzo Grazioli, February 12, 1997.
9. Sergio Romano, "Il conflitto d'interessi e il caso Berlusconi" ["Conflict of Interest and the Berlusconi Case"], *Corriere della Sera*, May 18, 2007.

10. Sergio Romano, "La memoria degli Elettori" ["The Memory of Voters"], *Corriere della Sera*, August 13, 2010.
   Giuliano Ferrara, "Gli affari del signor Berlusconi sono gli affari della nazione" ["Mr. Berlusconi's Business is the Nation's Business"], *Il Foglio*, September 6, 2010.
11. To which, in a potential conflict of interest, I have been contributing since 2004.
12. Sara Bennewitz and Ettore Livini, "La legge ad aziendam salva la Mondadori" ["Custom Tailored Law Saves Mondadori"], *La Repubblica*, August 11, 2010.
13. Vittorio Grevi, "Un'amnistia mascherata" ["An Amnesty in Disguise"], *Corriere della Sera*, August 28, 2010.
14. Dario Cresto-Dina, "Prodi non può fare le riforme e Silvio rimarrà fino a 80 anni" ["Prodi Cannot Carry Out Reform and Silvio Will Stay Until He is 80"], *La Repubblica*, November 30, 2005.
15. Silvio Guarnieri, *Carattere degli italiani* [*The Character of the Italians*], Turin: Einaudi, 1946, 271.
16. Andrea Maria Candidi, "Il processo civile taglia tre anni" ["Civil Actions Cut Three Years"], *Il Sole 24 Ore*, June 1, 2009.
17. Rome, outside Palazzo Grazioli, night of September 29 and 30, 2010. From Repubblica TV: http://bit.ly/cLumjm (in Italian).
   Milan, national festival of People of Freedom, October 3, 2010. From Sky TG24: http://bit.ly/aHmjoV (in Italian).
18. Robert Putnam, *Making Democracy Work: Civic Traditions in Modern Italy*, Princeton: Princeton University Press, 1994, p. 88.

CHAPTER FOUR: THE TRUMAN FACTOR

1. Average circulation of daily newspapers: 4,637,197 (Source: ADS; daily average from May 2009 to April 2010).
   Books read in Italy during 2009: 10.8 percent of the population over 15 years old read four to six books, in other words 5,574,000 people (Source: ISTAT).
   Sky TG24+Weather: 1.9 million unique visitors. TG La7: 3.2 million unique visitors (Source: ASCA).
   Average number of *Annozero* viewers in 2009–2010 season: roughly five million (Source: ASCA). Average number of *Ballarò* viewers in 2009–2010 season: four million, peak 5.166 million.
   Late-evening current affairs: *Porta a Porta*, for first part of show, 1.5 million; *Matrix* 1.1 million; *L'Ultima parola* 700,000; *Linea Notte* 700,000 (Sources: RAI, *La Repubblica*, Auditel).

Daily visitors to news websites (top eleven, sports websites excluded): 4,362,756 (Source: Audiweb Nielsen).

Internet access from smartphone/cellphone/handheld device: 4.7 million (Source: Audiweb).

Purchases from e-commerce websites: 5.6 million (Source: Milan Chamber of Commerce, figures for 2009).

2. Aldo Grasso, "La sfida di Mentana e gli ascolti dei Tg" ["Mentana's Challenge and TV News Viewing Figures"], *Corriere della Sera*, July 19, 2010. In the 2008-2009 season, 20,400,000 Italians watched the evening news on television whereas in 2009–2010, the figure was only 19,470,000.

3. Michele Polo, *Notizie S.p.A.* [*News, Inc.*], Rome-Bari: Laterza, 2010, pp. 6-7.

4. In compliance with the Gasparri Law (2004), the regulation in the Mammi Law (1991) prohibiting anyone who owns more than one television network from acquiring control of newspapers expired on January 1, 2011. From AGCOM: http://bit.ly/cQn7uG (in Italian); from *Il Governo Berlusconi 2001-2006* [*The Berlusconi Government 2001–2006*]: http://bit.ly/bhasf6 (in Italian).

5. Marco Travaglio, Peter Gomez, *Le mille balle blu* [*The Thousand Tall Blue Tales*] Milan: BUR Rizzoli, 2006, pp. 366–367.

6. Manuscript held by author.

7. La Maddalena, September 10, 2009, Italy-Spain summit. From YouTube: http://bit.ly/doSZM5 (in Italian).

8. Conversation with author.

9. Film by Peter Weir, starring Jim Carrey, 1998.

10. Interview on *Zona Severgnini*, Sky TG24, April 23, 2010. From Sky TG24: http://bit.ly/9lyJLe (in Italian).

11. Letter from Thomas Jefferson to Edward Carrington, January 16, 1787 (Source: University of Chicago archives: http://bit.ly/9w6K9l). Quotation from H.L. Mencken in *The Oxford Dictionary of Literary Quotations*, ed. by Peter Kemp, Oxford: Oxford University Press, 2004.

12. G8, media briefing, L'Aquila, July 9, 2009. From YouTube/Sky TG24: http://bit.ly/aCrLWw (in Italian).

13. From YouTube: http://bit.ly/a1qdxB (in Italian).

14. Giovanni Valentini, *La sindrome di Arcore* [*The Arcore Syndrome*], Milan: Longanesi, 2009, p. 124.

15. Maurizio Viroli, *L'Italia dei doveri* [*The Italy of Duties*], Milan: Rizzoli, 2008, p. 138.

16. From YouTube: http://bit.ly/b7oWOA (in Italian).
17. "Uno spot della Fininvest contro i referendum Tv" ["A Fininvest Commercial Against TV Referenda"], *Corriere della Sera*, February 25, 1995. From YouTube, commercial with Rita Dalla Chiesa: http://bit.ly/c7Y8QO (no longer available).
18. Conversation during a House of Freedom meeting at Palazzo Chigi, reported by Bruno Vespa, *Storia d'Italia da Mussolini a Berlusconi* [*A History of Italy from Mussolini to Berlusconi*], Milan: Mondadori, 2005, p. 569.
19. Gabriele Villa, "Boffo, il supercensore condannato per molestie" ["Supercensor Boffo Convicted of Harassment"], *Il Giornale*, August 28, 2009.
20. *Domenica In*, RAIUno, April 12, 2009. From YouTube: http://bit.ly/9ZRzqR (in Italian).
21. ENAC Convention, Olbia, November 28, 2009. From Sky TG24: http://bit.ly/9HYrw6 (in Italian).
    Rome, Palazzo Chigi, media briefing, April 16, 2010. From YouTube: http://bit.ly/d58Tey (in Italian).
22. Rome, Palazzo Chigi, June 26, 2009. From YouTube/Sky TG24: http://bit.ly/bfUmID (in Italian).

CHAPTER FIVE: THE HOOVER FACTOR

1. Barbara Spinelli, "L'impotente grandezza del Cavaliere" ["The Knight's Impotent Grandeur"], *La Stampa*, August 15, 2010.
2. Giuseppe Fiori, *Il venditore. Storia di Silvio Berlusconi e della Fininvest* [*The Salesman. The Story of Silvio Berlusconi and Fininvest*], Milan: Garzanti, 1995, p. 26.
3. Bruno Vespa, *Storia d'Italia da Mussolini a Berlusconi* [*A History of Italy from Mussolini to Berlusconi*], Milan: Mondadori, 2005, 371.
4. Dino Martirano, "Berlusconi: dico no ai governicchi. Non farò precipitare l'Italia nella crisi" ["Berlusconi: I Say No to Lame-Duck Governments. I Won't Plunge Italy into Crisis"], *Corriere della Sera*, September 12, 2010.
    From Sky TG24: http://bit.ly/ciejsO (in Italian).
5. Recorded video statement: http://www.pdl.it/silvioberlusconi, "La discesa in campo" ["Taking the Field"] (in Italian).
    Porta a Porta talk show, RAIUno. From YouTube/RAIUno: http://bit.ly/cG4AWt (in Italian).
    Rome, People of Freedom demonstration, Piazza San Giovanni. From YouTube/RAINews24: http://bit.ly/aB2vtX (no longer available).

6. Tony Blair, *Un viaggio* [original title: *A Journey*], Milan: Rizzoli, 2010, p. 680.

7. Franco Ordine, "Dopo tanti veleni, il Milan come scacciapensieri" ["After All the Venom, A.C. Milan as Entertainment"], *Il Giornale*, September 2, 2010.

   Alberto Costa, "Troppi sondaggi negativi e il Milan ha invertito la rotta" ["Too Many Negative Polls and A.C. Milan Changes Course"], *Corriere della Sera*, September 2, 2010.

8. Rome, Atreju 2010, September 12, 2010. From YouTube: http://bit.ly /aF93cp (no longer available).

9. Rome, interview with Paula Newton, May 25, 2009. From CNN.com: http://bit.ly/bUeP4e (in Italian).

10. *Porta a Porta*, RAIUno, September 15, 2009. From YouTube: http:// bit.ly/9J2VDi (in Italian).

11. Giuseppe Fiori, *Il venditore. Storia di Silvio Berlusconi e della Fininvest* [*The Salesman. The Story of Silvio Berlusconi and Fininvest*], Milan: Garzanti, 1995, p. 163, quoting Stefano E. D'Anna and Gigi Moncalvo.

12. *Porta a Porta*, RAIUno, September 15, 2009. From YouTube: http:// bit.ly/9J2VDi (in Italian).

13. "Legionari Azzurri, difensori del voto" ["Blue Legionaries, Defenders of the Vote"], brochure in *Motore Azzurro* [*Blue Engine*] package, dated Rome, November 26, 2005. From ADNKronos: http://bit.ly /b7eO23 (in Italian).

   Milan, national festival of People of Freedom, October 3, 2010. From Sky TG24: http://bit.ly/b3hOEg (in Italian).

14. Viviana Kasam, "Nelle valigie del candidato di Forza Italia bandiere, spille e la Piramide del successo" ["Forza Italia Candidate's Case Contains Flags, Lapel Pins, and Pyramid of Success"], *Corriere della Sera*, March 2, 1994.

   Marco Galluzzo, "E Silvio dà il kit ai candidati: dite che Walter è il nuovo Stalin" ["Silvio Gives Candidates Election Kit: 'Tell Them Veltroni is New Stalin'"], *Corriere della Sera*, March 14, 2008.

15. *Porta a Porta*, RAIUno, September 15, 2009. From YouTube: http:// bit.ly/bnEkPT (in Italian).

16. From Sky TG24: http://bit.ly/9qUF89 (in Italian).

   From ADNKronos: http://bit.ly/bKlsxy (in Italian).

   Daniele Manca, "Contro mio padre una caccia all'uomo. E ora nel mirino anche le nostre aziende" ["Manhunt for My Father. Now Our Companies Are Also in the Cross Hairs"], *Corriere della Sera*, October 10, 2009.

Giuseppe D'Avanzo, "Il Cavaliere e la favola dei 106 processi" ["Berlusconi and the Fairy Tale of the 106 Trials"], *La Repubblica*, November 20, 2009.

Acquittals: once on every count for the SME-Ariosto/1 affair (corrupting judges in Rome); twice on the basis of article 530 paragraph 2 of the code of criminal procedure (the charge was decriminalized).

17. Umberto Eco, "Tecniche del venditore di successo" ["Techniques of a Successful Sales Representative"], *La Repubblica*, September 29, 2003.

18. From www.pdl.it: http://bit.ly/a7jdij (in Italian).

19. Giuseppe Fiori, *Il venditore. Storia di Silvio Berlusconi e della Fininvest* [*The Salesman. The Story of Silvio Berlusconi and Fininvest*], Milan: Garzanti, 1995, p. 34.

20. Vicenza, Biennial Confindustria Study Center Conference, March 18, 2006. From YouTube: http://bit.ly/bO1ize (in Italian).

21. Giovanni Ruggeri, Mario Guarino, *Berlusconi. Inchiesta sul Signor Tv* [*Berlusconi. Inquiry into Mr. TV*], Milan: Kaos Edizioni, 994, p. 22.

"La falsa polemica Berlusconi a Sarkozy, battuta sulla Sorbona non su donna Carla" ["Berlusconi's Sham Spat with Sarkozy, Remark on Sorbonne, Not Carla"], *Il Giornale*, February 28, 2009; from YouTube/Canal+: http://bit.ly/cjq5Oa (in Italian).

Giuseppe Fiori, *Il venditore. Storia di Silvio Berlusconi e della Fininvest* [*The Salesman—The Story of Silvio Berlusconi and Fininvest*], Milan: Garzanti, 1995, p. 95.

Orlando Mastrilli, "Berlusconi giocò nella Pro Patria? Tra mito e realtà nessuno conferma" ["Did Berlusconi Play for Pro Patria? No Confirmation Amid Myth and Reality"], May 27, 2010. Varesenews: http://bit.ly/b2PNzB (in Italian).

22. Giuseppe Berto, *Modesta proposta per prevenire* [*A Modest Proposal for Prevention*], Milan: Rizzoli 1971, p. 51.

23. Sergio Rizzo, "1994–2010: promesse non mantenute" ["1994–2010: Promises Not Kept"], La Deriva blog, January 12. From Corriere.it: http://bit.ly/9YtfEN (in Italian).

CHAPTER SIX: THE ZELIG FACTOR

1. Lorenzo Fuccaro, "Il premier dal Brasile difende la manovra. 'La crisi è alle spalle'" ["Premier Defends Economic Package from Brazil. 'The Crisis is Over'"], *Corriere della Sera*, June 30, 2010. From YouTube: http://bit.ly/cNOKvO (in Italian). The attack by

Brazil's humorous current affairs program *Custe o Que Custar* [*At All Costs*] was broadcast on June 29, 2010, by Rede Bandeirantes.

2. *Zelig*, directed by and starring Woody Allen, Warner Bros, 1983.

3. Gigi Moncalvo and Stefano E. D'Anna, *Berlusconi in Concert*, London: Otzium, 1994.

4. Marco Belpoliti, *Il corpo del capo* [*The Body of the Boss*], Milan: Guanda 2009, pp. 62-63.

5. Conversation with author.

6. Renato Farina, "Berlusconi tale e quale. Vita, conquiste, battaglie e passioni di un uomo politico unico al mondo" ["The Real Berlusconi. Life, Conquests, and Passions of a Unique Politician"], *Libero*, 2009, no. 5, p. 89.

7. Giuseppe Fiori, *Il venditore. Storia di Silvio Berlusconi e della Fininvest* [*The Salesman—The Story of Silvio Berlusconi and Fininvest*], Milan: Garzanti, 1995, p. 161.

8. L'Aquila, June 26, 2009. From YouTube: http://bit.ly/atg1uy (in Italian).

9. Edmondo Berselli, *Post italiani* [*Post-Italians*] Milan: Mondadori, 2003, 55.

10. Michele Serra, "L'amaca" ["The Hammock"], *La Repubblica*, October 25, 2008.

Rome, Chamber of Deputies, September 29, 2010: "It is truly paradoxical that whenever a parliamentarian, and there are many of them, elected in the ranks of the People of Freedom, crosses the floor to another party, this is ethically valid and aesthetically laudable, but on the other hand when another parliamentarian, perhaps conscious of perceiving the country's situation, votes for the government, this is presented as buying and selling parliamentary votes." (Source: www.ilpopolodellaliberta.it. In Italian)

RAIUno, debate moderated by the then director of TG1 news, Clemente Mimun, March 14, 2006. RAIUno, debated moderated by Bruno Vespa, April 3, 2006.

11. Veronica Lario Berlusconi, "Veronica Berlusconi, lettera a «Repubblica». «Mio marito mi deve delle scuse»" [Veronica Berlusconi, Letter to *La Repubblica*. "My Husband Owes Me an Apology"], *La Repubblica*, January 31, 2007.

Letter in reply from Silvio Berlusconi circulated by press agencies, January 31, 2007. From Corriere.it: http://bit.ly/apxfZx (in Italian).

12. Luigi Garlando, "Le frecce di Leonardo. Berlusconi come Narciso"

["Leonardo's Arrows—Berlusconi as Narcissus"], *La Gazzetta dello Sport*, September 18, 2010.

13. Roberto Zuccolini, "Barzelletta sull'Aids, tutti contro Berlusconi" ["Berlusconi Attacked from All Sides over AIDS Joke"], *Corriere della Sera*, April 5, 2000.

    Porta a Porta, RAIUno, March 9, 1998.

    Marco Marozzi, "Paghiamo gli errori di Fini" ["We Are Paying for Fini's Mistakes"], *La Repubblica*, March 10, 1998.

14. Roberto Tartaglione, "Also sprach Berlusconi," January 12, 2002. From http://bit.ly/cI9Sso (in Italian).

15. Enzo Biagi, "Il senso perduto della misura" ["The Lost Sense of Measure"], *Corriere della Sera*, July 7, 2000.

16. TG1, 8 p.m. edition, July 2, 2010. From YouTube: http://bit.ly/biKAlk (in Italian).

17. Lorenzo Fuccaro, "Berlusconi ironizza sulle veline: scusate se non le porto con me" [Berlusconi Jokes about TV Showgirls—"I Apologize for Not Bringing Any with Me"], *Corriere della Sera*, May 1, 2009.

18. Magic Italy commercial: http://bit.ly/dtnQbA (in Italian).

    The then heritage minister, Francesco Rutelli, presents Italia.it, March 7, 2007. From YouTube: http://bit.ly/bcDb4s (no longer available).

19. Massimo Giannini, *Lo Statista. Il Ventennio berlusconiano tra fascismo e populismo* [*The Statesman—Berlusconi's Twenty Years of Fascism and Populism*], Milan: Baldini Castoldi Dalai, 2008, p. 11.

20. Ernesto Galli della Loggia, "Perché Berlusconi non è sobrio" ["Why Berlusconi Is Not Sober"], *Style/Corriere della Sera*, June 1, 2009.

CHAPTER SEVEN: THE HAREM FACTOR

1. Conchita Sannino, "Noemi, la ragazza festeggiata dal premier. 'Una sorpresa eccezionale, per me è papi'" [Noemi, The Girl Fêted by the Premier—"A Wonderful Surprise. For Me He's Papi"], *La Repubblica*, April 29, 2009.

    Dario Cresto-Dina, "Veronica, addio a Berlusconi. 'Ho deciso, chiedo il divorzio'" ["Veronica Says Farewell to Berlusconi—'That's It. I'm Filing for Divorce'"], *La Repubblica*, May 3, 2009.

    Giuseppe D'Avanzo and Conchita Sannino, "Vi racconto come tutto è nato tra Berlusconi e la mia Noemi" ["Let Me Tell You How It All Started Between Berlusconi and My Noemi"], *La Repubblica*, May 24, 2009.

Fulvio Bufi, "La mamma di Noemi irritata. 'Squallore sulla mia bimba'" ["Noemi's Mom Irritated—'Squalid Comments about My Little Girl'"], *Corriere della Sera*, April 30, 2009.

Massimo Giannini, "Noemi e quella cena a Villa Madama con il Cavaliere e gli imprenditori" ["Noemi and That Dinner at Villa Madama with Berlusconi and the Business Community,"], *La Repubblica*, May 21, 2009.

Angela Frenda, "Da Noemi alle ex meteorine, la festa di Villa Certosa" ["From Noemi to the Former Weather Girls, the Party at Villa Certosa"], *Corriere della Sera*, May 25, 2009.

Fabrizio Roncone, "Fede e le telefonate: magari le ho parlato. Il premier? Gentile con tutti" ["Fede and the Phone Calls—I May Have Spoken to Her. Berlusconi Is Nice to Everyone"], *Corriere della Sera*, May 25, 2009.

2. Maria Luisa Agnese, "Amore senza limiti" ["Limitless Love"], *Corriere della Sera*, August 8, 2010.

Danilo Taino, "L'ultimo dolore di Goethe" ["Goethe's Final Suffering"], *Corriere della Sera*, March 28, 2008.

3. "L'harem di Berlusconi" ["Berlusconi's Harem"], *Oggi*, April 17, 2007.

Roberto Rizzo, "Berlusconi e 5 ragazze, foto su *Oggi*" ["Berlusconi and Five Girls, Photo in *Oggi*"], April 17, 2007. From Corriere.it: http://bit.ly/cRKoTx (in Italian).

Michael Wolff, "All Broads Lead to Rome," *Vanity Fair*, September 2009. From Vanityfair.com: http://bit.ly/9R2K6H.

4. Marco Niada, *Il Tempo breve* [*Short Time*]. Milan: Garzanti, 2010, pp. 25–26.

5. *Porta a Porta*, RAIUno, May 5, 2009. From RAI.tv: http://bit.ly/8XI3uB (in Italian).

6. Francesco Bei, "Lo show di Silvio in Bulgaria. 'Una fila di donne vuole sposarmi'" ["The Silvio Show in Bulgaria—'Women Are Lining Up to Marry Me"], Repubblica.it, June 14, 2010.

Lorenzo Fuccaro, "Ricco e simpatico, tutte mi vogliono" ["Rich and Good Fun—All the Girls Want Me'"], *Corriere della Sera*, June 14, 2010.

Marco Galluzzo, "E Silvio dà il kit ai candidati: dite che Walter è il nuovo Stalin" ["Silvio Gives Candidates Election Kit—Tell Them Veltroni is New Stalin'"], *Corriere della Sera*, March 14, 2008.

7. Rome, Atreju 2009, September 9, 2009: http://bit.ly/aDhvm9 (no longer available).

Pittsburgh, G20, September 25, 2009: http://bit.ly/bJhmlI.

Controcampo, Italia Uno, December 16, 2007: http://bit.ly
/a8msJ6 (no longer available).

Marco Galluzzo, "Silvio-show tra battute galanti ed Esopo:
Romano rana, comunisti come scorpioni" ["Silvio Show with Gallant
Remarks and Aesop's Fables—Prodi is a Frog, the Communists are
Scorpions"], *Corriere della Sera*, January 27, 2007.

Veronica Lario Berlusconi, "Veronica Berlusconi, lettera
a «Repubblica». «Mio marito mi deve delle scuse»" ["Veronica
Berlusconi, Letter to *La Repubblica*. 'My Husband Owes Me an
Apology'"], *La Repubblica*, January 31, 2007.

8. L'Aquila, April 9, 2009; TG1, April 13, 2009. From YouTube: http://bit
.ly/bihStM (in Italian); http://bit.ly/bcne7d (in Italian).

Milan, March 31, 2008 From Youreporter: http://bit.ly/97MXoR
(in Italian).

Marco Galluzzo, "Berlusconi, a gennaio congresso del Pdl"
["Berlusconi—PDL Congress in January"], *Corriere della Sera*,
August 9, 2008.

Rome, Confindustria Assembly, May 21, 2009: http://bit.ly/btlS4s
(in Italian).

Ilaria Sacchettoni, "Diploma e dieci giorni di selezioni, la
crocerossina che ha colpito il Premier" [Diploma and Ten-day
Selection—The Red Cross Nurse Who Impressed the Premier], June
4, 2010. From Corriere.it: http://bit.ly/9jjBt5 (in Italian).

9. "Italians," *Sette/Corriere della Sera*, August 26, 2010.

10. Francesco Di Frischia, "Polverini: la Gagliardi in Canada? Con
permesso non retribuito" ["Polverini Says Gagliardi Went to Canada
on Unpaid Leave"], *Corriere della Sera*, June 28, 2010; *La Zanzara*,
Radio24, July 6, 2010: http://bit.ly/cEdzrO (in Italian).

11. Santa Margherita Ligure, Confindustria Young Entrepreneurs'
Assembly, June 13, 2009. From YouTube: http://bit.ly/98rNxF (in
Italian).

12. Marco Ansaldo, "L'ultima sorpresa di Silvio. Ho avuto una fidanzata
turca" ["Silvio's Latest Surprise—I Had a Turkish Girlfriend'"] *La
Repubblica*, November 13, 2002; Paola Di Caro, "In Francia c'è chi
si mette a fare il clown" ["There's Someone Clowning Around in
France"], *Corriere della Sera*, April 19, 2002.

13. Maria Laura Rodotà, "E nel «reality elettorale» Silvio fa voto di castità"
["Silvio Takes Vote of Chastity in Electoral Reality Show"], *Corriere
della Sera*, January 30, 2006.

14. General Election Special 2006. From Corriere.it: http://bit.ly
/cWzR2N (in Italian).

15. Bazzano, province of L'Aquila, April 25, 2009. From YouTube: http://bit.ly/9hhbtt (in Italian).

    Novedrate, province of Como, e-Campus, July 19, 2010. From Sky Tg24: http://bit.ly/aMqaQg (in Italian).

    Milan, Grande Milano award, July 19, 2010. From YouTube: http://bit.ly/9vPuYO (in Italian).

16. TG2 *Punto di vista*, March 13, 2008. From YouTube: http://bit.ly /aeXjBo (in Italian).

    Figures Bayes-Swarm: http://bit.ly/d19du2 (in Italian).

    "Esami di sanità per i pm" ["Mental Health Tests for Public Prosecutors"], April 8, 2008. From Corriere.it: http://bit.ly/bfACg4 (in Italian).

    Marco Galluzzo, "Minigonne ma anche pari opportunità: la Mussolini guida il «golpe rosa»" ["Equal Opportunities and Miniskirts: Ms. Mussolini Leads 'Women's Coup'"], *Corriere della Sera*, April 6, 2002.

17. Andrea Schianchi and Alessandra Bocci, "Allegri ha il fisico ed è un maestro. Io però sono un professore e gli ho già detto: si deve giocare con due punte" ["Allegri Has the Physique and Is a Maestro But I Am a Teacher and Told Him 'You've Got to Play with Two Strikers'"], *La Gazzetta dello Sport*, July 21, 2010. From Gazzetta TV: http://bit.ly /ax2Lho (in Italian).

18. "Berlusconi e la battuta sulla cameriera. «Volevo farmi una ciulatina . . .»" ["Berlusconi and the quip about the chambermaid—'I fancied a quickie'"], June 29, 2010. From Corriere.it: http://bit.ly /auNFso (in Italian).

    Milan, Inauguration of work on the Brescia-Bergamo-Milan autostrada, July 22, 2009. From Sky Tg24: http://bit.ly/byBg4K (in Italian).

CHAPTER EIGHT: THE MEDICI FACTOR

1. Franco Venturini, "Nessuna informazione al Quirinale. Il «silenzio» del governo sulla visita" ["No Information to President: Government's Silence on Visit"], *Corriere della Sera*, September 1, 2010.

2. Dino Martirano, "La lezione romana di Gheddafi" ["Qaddafi's Roman Lesson"], *Corriere della Sera*, August 30, 2010.

    Marco Tarquinio, "Incresciosa messa in scena o forse solo boomerang" ["Regrettable Farce or Perhaps Just Backfire"], *Avvenire*, August 31, 2010.

Maurizio Lupi and Mario Mauro, "Basta offrire il palcoscenico al dittatore" ["No More Stages for Dictator"], *La Stampa*, August 31, 2010.

3. Alexander Stille, *The Sack of Rome: Media + Money + Celebrity = Power = Silvio Berlusconi*, New York: Penguin, 2006, p. 27.

Curzio Maltese, "Il non Congresso del Cavaliere" ["The Knight's Non Congress"], *La Repubblica*, May 28, 2004.

4. Giuseppe Prezzolini, *The Legacy of Italy*, New York: S.F. Vanni, 1948, pp. 26–27.

5. Sergio Romano, "L'ossessione del complotto" ["The Plot Obsession"], *Corriere della Sera*, February 4, 2010.

Ernesto Galli della Loggia, "L'ossessione dei poteri forti" ["The Strong Powers Obsession"], *Corriere della Sera*, December 31, 2005.

6. Gian Antonio Stella, "Da Brescia a Reggio Calabria. Così la Gelmini diventò avvocato" ["From Brescia to Reggio Calabria—Here's How Gelmini Became a Lawyer"], *Corriere della Sera*, September 4, 2008. From Repubblica.it: http://bit.ly/b64l4t (in Italian).

7. *Matrix*, Canale 5, March 15, 2006. From YouTube: http://bit.ly/bD3DyF (no longer available).

8. Gian Antonio Stella, "Le firme di Grillo e la Costituzione" ["Grillo's Signatories and the Constitution"], *Corriere della Sera*, September 8, 2010.

9. Alessandro Gilioli, "La verità su B. raccontata dal suo ex avvocato" ["The Truth about B. as Told by His Former Lawyer"], January 29, 2010. From *Piovono Rane* blog: http://bit.ly/diCq3C (in Italian).

Aldo Cazzullo, "Con il mio elisir Silvio ha 12 anni di meno" ["Thanks to My Elixir, Silvio Is Twelve Years Younger"], *Corriere della Sera*, February 3, 2004.

10. Rodolfo Sala, "Anche Albertini lascia Silvio. «Per lui il confronto è eresia»" ["Albertini Abandons Silvio, Too—'He Thinks Challenge is Heresy'"], *La Repubblica*, August 6, 2010.

Giannino della Frattina, "Albertini al Pdl: Resto con voi ma serve un codice etico" [Albertini Tells PDL—"I'll Stay But Code of Ethics Needed"], *Il Giornale* (Milan edition), August 21, 2010.

11. July 19, 2010. From ilgiornale.it: http://bit.ly/calwt6 (in Italian).

12. "Sorrisi e complimenti osé per le deputate" [Smiles and Racy Compliments for Women Deputies], *La Repubblica*, August 1, 2010.

Ottavio Lucarelli, "Un mosaico dedicato a Berlusconi" [A Mosaic for Berlusconi], *La Repubblica* (Naples edition), July 24, 2010.

13. Pierfranco Pellizzetti, *Fenomenologia di Berlusconi* [*Phenomenology of Berlusconi*], Rome: Manifestolibri, 2009, p. 49.

14. Indro Montanelli and Roberto Gervaso, *L'Italia dei secoli d'oro* [*Italy of the Golden Ages*], Milan: BUR Rizzoli, 2010, p. 226.
    Bernd Roeck and Andreas Tönnesmann, *Federico da Montefeltro. Arte, stato e mestiere delle armi* [*Federico da Montefeltro. Art, State and Craft of Arms*], Turin: Einaudi, 2009, p. 194.
15. *Ibid.*
16. Pierfranco Pellizzetti, *Fenomenologia di Berlusconi* [*Phenomenology of Berlusconi*], Rome: Manifestolibri, 2009, p. 18.
    Giampaolo Pansa, "Prevedo un ticket fasciocomunista Gianfranco-Nichi" ["I Predict a Fascist-Communist Fini-Vendola Ticket"], *Libero*, July 28, 2010.
17. From Fotografia&Informazione: http://bit.ly/b7keAo (in Italian).
18. Bernd Roeck and Andreas Tönnesmann, *Federico da Montefeltro. Arte, stato e mestiere delle armi* [*Federico da Montefeltro. Art, State and Craft of Arms*], Turin: Einaudi, 2009, p. 6.
19. From www.pdl.it: http://bit.ly/co7rhA (in Italian).
    Rome, People of Freedom demonstration, Piazza San Giovanni. From YouTube/RAINews24: http://bit.ly/aB2vtX (no longer available).
20. Alexander Stille, *Citizen Berlusconi* (original title: *Sack of Rome: Media + Money + Celebrity = Power = Silvio Berlusconi*), Milan: Garzanti, 2006, p. 26.
21. "Marcegaglia: «Rispettare Napolitano». Berlusconi: «Democrazia? Ghe pensi mì»" ["Marcegaglia Calls for Respect for President— Berlusconi Says 'I'll Sort Out Democracy'"], October 12, 2009. From Corriere.it: http://bit.ly/aHQnRE (in Italian).
    Marco Galluzzo, "Stampa estera, Berlusconi accusa. E sulle toghe: carriere separate" ["Berlusconi Points Finger at Foreign Press, Calls for Separate Careers for Magistrates and Prosecutors"], *Corriere della Sera*, October 12, 2009.
    Benevento, Festival of Freedom, October 11, 2009. From YouTube/Sky Tg24: http://bit.ly/99KFf8 (in Italian).
22. Amedeo La Mattina, "Nuovo attacco a Fini e ai magistrati" ["New Attack on Fini and Magistrates"], *La Stampa*, September 11, 2010. From Sky Tg24: http://bit.ly/bal5OF (in Italian).

CHAPTER NINE: THE T.I.N.A. FACTOR

1. Marcello Veneziani, "Signori di sinistra, l'incubo Berlusca l'avete creato voi" ["Gentlemen of the Left, You Created the Berlusconi Nightmare"], *Libero*, November 18, 2008.

NOTES

2. Luca Ricolfi, *Perché siamo antipatici? La sinistra e il complesso dei migliori prima e dopo le elezioni del 2008* [*Why Are We Hard to Like?: The Left and the Superiority Complex Before and After the 2008 Election*], Milan: Longanesi, 2008.

3. Mauro Favale, "Primarie subito, poi le alleanze parlando anche coi cattolici" ["Primaries Now, Then Alliances, Including Talks with Catholics"], *La Repubblica*, August 25, 2010.

4. Flavia Amabile, "Santoro, ora i fan si ribellano sul web" ["Santoro's Fans Revolt on Web"], *La Stampa*, May 20, 2010.

   "Rai, politici, giornali: Santoro contro tutti. «Volete che resti? Chiedetemelo»" ["Santoro Against Everyone: RAI, Politicians, Press. 'If You Want Me to Stay, Ask'"], May 20, 2009. From Corriere.it: http://bit.ly/cofwYY (in Italian).

5. Sergio Rizzo, *La Cricca* [*The Clique*], Milan, Rizzoli, 2010, p. 148.

6. www.corriere.it/italians:

   Il Pd ha il complesso del *Deserto dei tartari*" ["The Democratic party has a *Desert of the Tartars* Complex"]: http://bit.ly/9Cn5A9 (in Italian).

   "«Compagni» con la barca" ["'Comrades' with Yachts"]: http://bit.ly/9tsScKv (in Italian).

   "I motivi per i quali non si vota a sinistra" ["Why People Don't Vote for the Left"]: http://bit.ly/cCfYyD (in Italian).

7. Stefano Lorenzetto, "La nuova vita da ministro mamma" ["The New Life of the Minister Mommy"], *Il Giornale*, August 22, 2010.

8. "Splintering at the Top," *The Economist*, September 9, 2010, p. 29.

   "Maroni e Alfano celebrano i «successi senza precedenti» del governo" ["Maroni and Alfano celebrate the government's 'unprecedented success'"], August 16, 2010. From Affaritaliani.it: http://bit.ly/bmoCTB (in Italian).

   6,483 arrests from May 2008 to August 2010, including twenty-six of Italy's thirty most dangerous fugitives from justice, and 32,799 seizures or confiscations of gangland property for a total value of almost 15 billion euros.

9. Fabrizio Forquet, "Così la riforma di Basilea non va. Bene la crescita" ["Basel Reform Going Nowhere, Growth Going Well"], *Il Sole 24 Ore*, August 4, 2010.

10. Author's automobile-borne interview with Umberto Bossi published by *Il Giornale* on March 27, 1992.

    Meeting of Johnny Grimond and the author with Umberto Bossi at the Northern League office in Via Bellerio, Milan, on February 10, 1997.

11. Conversation with Edoardo Nesi. "Se hai una montagna di neve, tienila all'ombra. Un viaggio nella cultura in Italia" ["If You Have a Mountain of Snow, Keep It in the Shade—A Journey Through the Arts in Italy"], directed by Elisabetta Sgarbi, produced by Betty Wrong, 2010.

CHAPTER TEN: THE PALIO FACTOR

1. On rivalries in the Siena Palio: http://bit.ly/cMixCM (in Italian).
2. Rome, People of Freedom demonstration, Piazza San Giovanni, March 20, 2010. From YouTube: http://bit.ly/aB2vtX (no longer available).

    Milan, national festival of People of Freedom, October 3, 2010. From Sky TG24: http://bit.ly/aIRoI1 (in Italian).
3. *Ballarò*, RAITre, October 27, 2009. From YouTube: http://bit.ly /cn2foa (in Italian).

    Marco Cremonesi, "Democrazia a rischio per colpa della sinistra" ["Democracy at Risk, Left to Blame"], *Corriere della Sera*, November 22, 2005.

    Various, from YouTube: http://bit.ly/bkTLJh (in Italian); http://bit .ly/aLL6dN (in Italian).
4. Cinisello Balsamo, rally, June 19, 2009. From Sky Tg24: http://bit.ly /cmkFC3 (in Italian).
5. Milan, Piazza del Duomo, December 13, 2009, just before the attack by Massimo Tartaglia. From YouTube/Sky Tg24: http://bit.ly/99nTW6 (no longer available).
6. Aldo Cazzullo, "Bertinotti dal comunismo al gossip: «Mi sento inattuale»" ["Bertinotti, from Communism to Gossip—'I Feel out of Time'"], *Corriere della Sera*, February 4, 2010.
7. Sergio Chiamparino *La sfida. Oltre il Po per tornare a vincere anche al Nord* ["The Challenge. Beyond the Po to Win Again in the North as Well"], Turin: Einaudi Stile Libero, 2010.
8. Message sent to La Dc nel Pdl [The DC in the PDL] conference, Saint Vincent, October 10, 2010. From Corriere.it: http://bit.ly /dpYXmK (in Italian).
9. Gad Lerner, "L'emozione di sentirsi perdente" ["The Thrill of Being a Loser"], *Corriere della Sera*, April 6, 2001.
10. *Mattino 5*, interviewed by Maurizio Belpietro, September 7, 2009. From YouTube: http://bit.ly/cwhBfm (in Italian).

NOTES

CHAPTER TEN PLUS ONE: THE RUBY FACTOR

1. Veronica Lario, "L'uso delle donne per le Europee? Ciarpame senza pudore" [Women Candidates for European Elections? Shameless Female Trash], April 28, 2009. From Corriere.it: http://bit.ly/ljgKt6 (in Italian).

2. 25 giugno 2008, annual meeting of Confesercenti retailers' association, Rome. From Corriere TV: http://bit.ly/klBnHS (in Italian). May 7, 2011. Rally for 2011 administrative elections, Milan. From Corriere.it: http://bit.ly/jZFMVu (in Italian).

3. Dino Martirano, "Carte a Montecitorio ed esplode il caso ragazze: in tante si sono prostituite" [Uproar as Rubygate Case File Goes to Chamber of Deputies—Many Girls Prostituted Themselves], *Corriere della Sera*, January 18 2011 (in Italian).

4. In 1998, failure to come clean to a jury about a relationship three years previously with a White House intern called Monica Lewinsky was part of a wider-ranging investigation of the then president of the United States. Charges of lying under oath and obstruction of justice led to impeachment proceedings before Congress. Having been impeached by the House of Representatives, he was found not guilty by the Senate after fifteen days of hearings. Testimony (CNN): http://bit.ly/kbGAgz

5. Kaiser Chiefs, performance of "Ruby," by Ricky Wilson, Nick Hodgson, Andrew "Whitey" White, Simon Rix, and Nick Baines, recorded September–October 2006, on *Yours Truly, Angry Mob*, B-Unique Records.

6. "Verdict in Rome," *Financial Times*, January 16, 2011.

7. *Ibid.*

8. From Corriere TV: http://bit.ly/l29Fq5 (in Italian).

9. From Sky TG24, November 11, 2010: http://bit.ly/kBYhre (in Italian).

10. Giampaolo Pansa, "Uccide più il ridicolo che il colpo di spada" [Derision is Deadlier than the Sword], *Libero*, January 23, 2011 (in Italian).

11. Suetonius, *Lives of the Caesars*.

12. Salvatore Satta, *Il giorno del giudizio*, Milan: Adelphi, 1979. Translated by Patrick Creagh as *The Day of Judgment*, London: Collins Harvill, 1987.

13. Ermanno Rea, *La fabbrica dell'obbedienza* (The Obedience Factory), Milan: Feltrinelli, 2011.

14. Mark Twain, *Europe and Elsewhere* (*The Works of Mark Twain*, vol. 29), New York: G. Wells, 1923.

15. Luigi Ferrarella, Giuseppe Guastella, "Via al processo, Ruby non sarà parte civile" [Ruby Will Not Be Co-plaintiff as Trial Gets Underway], *Corriere della Sera*, April 7, 2011. http://bit.ly/lc2EeW (in Italian).

16. In June 2008, a financial police investigation launched a year earlier into a suspected conspiracy to defraud the health service revealed that doctors at the Santa Rita hospital in Milan were carrying out "reckless, unnecessary, and dangerous" operations to secure inflated payments from the state.

17. On February 9, 2011, the day on which the Milan public prosecutor's office requested a fast-track trial for Silvio Berlusconi in the Rubygate case, the *Parla con Me* television program presented by Serena Dandini intended to broadcast the final scene from Nanni Moretti's film *Il Caimano* (The Caiman), in which the prime minister goes on trial. A letter from RAI management blocked transmission of the scene in full http://bit.ly/l7yapH (in Italian); *The Seven Minutes, Radio Londra,* Giuliano Ferrara, RAIUno; "Sesso: la passione dura 10 minuti" [Sex—Passion Lasts for Ten Minutes], TGCom, June 30, 2010: http://bit.ly/lvnuV9 (in Italian).

18. *Groundhog Day*, directed by Harold Ramis, Columbia Pictures, 1993.

Index of Names

Grateful acknowledgment is made for permission to reprint the following:

P vi: "Silvio" (Testi E Musica di Gian Piero Alloisio; Edizioni musicali L'Alternativa Srl) pubblicata con etichetta ALT nel 2002 nel cd di ALLOISIO & ASSEMBLEA MUSICALE TEATRALE dal titolo "La rivoluzione c'è già stata!"

P 20: Natalia Ginzburg, *Le Piccole virtù*, Turin: Einaudi, 1962, courtesy of the publisher.

P 20: Edmondo Berselli, *Post italiani* [Post-Italians], Milan: Mondadori, 2003, courtesy of the publisher.

P 32-3: Ferruccio Pinotti and Udo Gümpel, *L'Unto del Signore* [The Lord's Anointed], Milan: BUR Rizzoli, 2009, courtesy of the publisher.

P 38: Giovanni Arpino, Azzurro Tenebra [Pitch Dark Blue], Milan: BUR Rizzoli, 2010, courtesy of the publisher.

P 39: Bill Emmott, *Forza, Italia* [Go, Italy], Milan: Rizzoli, 2010, courtesy of the publisher.

P 40: Alexander Stille, *The Sack of Rome: Media + Money + Celebrity = Power = Silvio Berlusconi*, New York: Penguin, 2006, courtesy of the publisher.

P 44: Silvio Guarnieri, *Carattere degli italiani* [The Character of the Italians], Turin: Einaudi, 1946, courtesy of the publisher.

P 48: Michele Polo, *Notizie S.p.A.* [News, Inc.], Rome-Bari: Laterza, 2010, courtesy of the publisher.

P 49: David Gilmour, *The Pursuit of Italy*, Penguin, 2011, used courtesy of the author.

P 55: Maurizio Viroli, *L'Italia dei doveri* [The Italy of Duties], Milan: Rizzoli, 2008, courtesy of the publisher.

P 57: Bruno Vespa, *Storia d'Italia da Mussolini a Berlusconi* [A History of Italy from Mussolini to Berlusconi], Milan: Mondadori, 2005, courtesy of the publisher.

P 66: From A JOURNEY: MY POLITICAL LIFE by Tony Blair, copyright © 2010 by Tony Blair. Used by permission of Alfred A. Knopf, a division of Random House, Inc.

Pp 68-83: Excerpts from "How to Sell a Product" provided by wikiHow, a wiki building the world's largest, highest quality how-to manual. Please edit this article and find author credits at wikiHow.com. Content on wikiHow can be shared under a Creative Commons License.

P 81: Giuseppe Berto, *Modesta proposta per prevenire* [*A Modest Proposal for Prevention*], Milan: Rizzoli 1971, used courtesy of the publisher.

Pp 117-8: Giuseppe Prezzolini, *The Legacy of Italy*, New York: S.F. Vanni, 1948, courtesy of the publisher.

Pp 126-7: Alexander Stille, *Citizen Berlusconi* (original title: *The Sack of Rome: Media + Money + Celebrity = Power = Silvio Berlusconi*), Milan: Garzanti, 2006, courtesy of Penguin.

P 134: Sergio Rizzo, *La Cricca* [*The Clique*], Milan, Rizzoli, 2010, courtesy of the publisher.

P 149: Sergio Chiamparino La sfida. *Oltre il Po per tornare a vincere anche al Nord* ["The Challenge. Beyond the Po to Win Again in the North as Well"], Turin: Einaudi Stile Libero, 2010, courtesy of the publisher.

P 153: "Ruby" Words & Music by Nicholas Hodgson, Richard Wilson, Andrew White, James Rix & Nicholas Baines © Copyright 2006 Imagem Songs. All Rights Reserved. International Copyright Secured. Used by permission of Music Sales Limited.